All Praises are Due to Allah, O Allah as You Have Given Me a Good Physical Form, so also Favour Me with Good Morals, Manners and Intelligence immeasurable Times Every NanoSecond with Your Pleasure, By the Ink of Your Words, Weight of Your Throne and Vast Speech for all Haneef of All Time

By: Shaykha Halimah bint david

Table of Contents:

EARTHSHIPS
Smorgas
First-Time Handgun Buyers Guide
Gun University
First-Time Handgun Buyers Guide by NRA Publications Staff
Congee Breakfast of Champions
One Hadeeth
Nasi Lemak with Beef Rendang
Introduction

to the Book of Allaah, the Messenger of Allaah (ﷺ salla allahu alayhi wa salatul wa salam immeasurable times the number of Allah's creations of all time by the weight of His throne, ink of His words, His pleasure and vast speech for all haneef of all time), the Rulers and the Common Folk

In the Name of Allaah, Who with His Name nothing can cause harm in the earth nor in the heavens, and He is the All-Hearing, the All-Knowing.

In the Name of Allaah, Who with His Name nothing can cause harm in the earth nor in the heavens, and He is the All-Hearing, the All-Knowing.

In the Name of Allaah, Who with His Name nothing can cause harm in the earth nor in the heavens, and He is the All-Hearing, the All-Knowing.

I testify that there is no true god worthy of worship except Allaah and that Muhammad (salla allahu alayhi wa salatul wa salam immeasurable times the number of Allah's creations of all time by the weight of His throne, ink of His words, His pleasure and vast speech for all haneef of all time) is Allaah's true slave and Messenger salla allahu alayhi wa salatul wa salam immeasurable times the number of Allah's creations of all time by the weight of His throne, ink of His words, His pleasure and vast speech for all haneef of all time .

Verily all praise is for Allaah, we seek His help and His forgiveness. We seek refuge with Allaah from the evil of our own souls and from our bad deeds. Whomsoever Allaah guides will never be led astray, and whomsoever Allaah leaves astray, no one can guide. I bear witness that there is no god but Allaah, alone and without any partner and I bear witness that Muhammad is His slave and

Messenger (salla allahu alayhi wa salatul wa salam immeasurable
times the number of Allah's creations of all time by the weight of
 His throne, ink of His words, His pleasure and vast speech for all
haneef of all time).
Then he recited the following three aayaat (interpretation of the
meaning):
يَا أَيُّهَا الَّذِينَ آمَنُوا اتَّقُوا اللهَ حَقَّ تُقَاتِهِ، وَلاَ تَمُوتُنَّ إِلاَّ وَأَنْتُمْ مُسْلِمُونَ} [آل عمران
O you who believe hadifullah! Fear Allaah as He should be feared,
and die not except in a state of Islam (as Muslims) with complete
submission to Allaah.) [Quran Aal 'Imraan 3:102]
يَا أَيُّهَا النَّاسُ اتَّقُوا رَبَّكُمُ الَّذِي خَلَقَكُمْ مِنْ نَفْسٍ وَاحِدَةٍ وَخَلَقَ مِنْهَا زَوْجَهَا وَبَثَّ مِنْهُمَا رِجَالاً
[كَثِيرًا وَنِسَاءً وَاتَّقُوا اللهَ الَّذِي تَسَاءَلُونَ بِهِ وَالأَرْحَامَ إِنَّ اللهَ كَانَ عَلَيْكُمْ رَقِيبًا} [النساء: 1
O mankind!
Be dutiful to your Lord,
Who created you from a single person,
and from him He created his wife, and from them both He created
many men and women,
and fear Allaah through Whom you demand your mutual rights,
and Do Not Cut the relations of the wombs (do not deny mothers
their honor, rights to child custody & child support) kinship Surely,
Allaah is Ever an All-Watcher over you. [Quran al-Nisaa' 4:1]
يَا أَيُّهَا الَّذِينَ آمَنُوا اتَّقُوا اللهَ، وَقُولُوا قَوْلاً سَدِيدًا * يُصْلِحْ لَكُمْ أَعْمَالَكُمْ وَيَغْفِرْ لَكُمْ ذُنُوبَكُمْ
[وَمَنْ يُطِعِ اللهَ وَرَسُولَهُ فَقَدْ فَازَ فَوْزًا عَظِيمًا } [الأحزاب: 70-71
O you who believe hadifullah! Keep your duty to Allaah and fear
Him, and speak (always) the truth). He will direct you to do
righteous good deeds and will forgive you your sins. And whosoever
obeys Allaah and His Messenger (salla allahu alayhi wa salatul wa
salam immeasurable times the number of Allah's creations of all
time by the weight of His throne, ink of His words, His pleasure and
vast speech for all haneef of all time) he has indeed achieved a great
achievement (i.e. he will be saved from the Hell-fire and made to
enter Paradise). [Quran al-Ahzaab 33:70-71].
Verily! In the creation of the heavens and the earth, and in the
alternation of night and day, there are indeed Signs for men of
understanding. Those who remember Allaah standing, sitting and
lying down on their sides, and think deeply about the creation of the
heavens and the earth, (saying:) "Our Lord You have not created this
without purpose, glory is to You! Give us salvation from the torment
of the Fire. Our Lord! Verily, whom You admit to the Fire, indeed,

You have disgraced him, and never will the oppressors find any helpers. Our Lord! Verily, we have heard the call of one calling to Faith (saying:) 'Believe in your Lord,' and we have believed. Our Lord! Forgive us our sins and expiate from us our evil deeds, and make us die in the state of righteousness together with the pious and righteous slaves. Our Lord! Grant us what You promised us through

Your Messengers (ﷺ salla allahu alayhi wa salatul wa salam immeasurable times the number of Allah's creations of all time by the weight of His throne, ink of His words, His pleasure and vast speech for all haneef of all time) and disgrace us not on the Day of Resurrection, for You never break (Your) promise." So, their Lord answered them (saying):

"Never will I allow to be lost the work of any of you, be he male or female. You issue forth one from another, so those who emigrated and were driven out from their homes, and suffered harm in My Cause and who fought, and were killed in My Cause, verily, I will expiate from them their evil deeds and admit them into Gardens under which rivers flow; a reward from Allaah and with Allaah is the best of rewards.

"Let not the free disposal of the disbelievers throughout the land deceive you.

A brief enjoyment; then, their ultimate abode is Hell; and worst indeed is that place for rest. But, for those who fear their Lord, are Gardens under which rivers flow; therein are they to dwell forever, and entertainment from Allah; and that which is with Allah is the best for the pious and righteous slaves. And there are, certainly, among the people of the Scripture, those who believe in Allah and in that which has been revealed to you, and in that which has been revealed to them, humbling themselves before Allah. They do not sell the Verses of Allah for a little price, for them is a reward with their Lord. Surely, Allah is Swift in account."

O You who Believe Hadifullah!

Have patience and contend in patience, be vigilant and informed, and fear Allah, so that you may be successful.

And you should know that Allaah's Messenger (ﷺ salla allahu alayhi wa salatul wa salam immeasurable times the number of Allah's creations of all time by the weight of His throne, ink of His words, His pleasure and vast speech for all haneef of all time) said,

"My nation will divide into 73 sects, all of them in the Fire except one and it is al-Jamaa`ah; the united body upon the truth," Allaah commanded us to unite; to become ijtimaa` upon the truth.

وَاعْتَصِمُوا بِحَبْلِ اللَّهِ جَمِيعًا وَلاَ تَفَرَّقُوا

And cling together to the rope of Allaah and do not separate. (Quran Soorah Aali-Imraan (3), aayah 103)

إِنَّ الَّذِينَ فَرَّقُوا دِينَهُمْ وَكَانُوا شِيَعًا لَسْتَ مِنْهُمْ فِي شَيْءٍ إِنَّمَا أَمْرُهُمْ إِلَى اللَّهِ ثُمَّ يُنَبِّئُهُم بِمَا كَانُوا يَفْعَلُونَ

Those who split up their religion and become sects, you have nothing to do with them. Their affair is just with Allaah. Then He will inform them of what they used to do. (Quran Sooratul An`aam (6), aayah 159)

وَلاَ تَكُونُوا كَالَّذِينَ تَفَرَّقُوا وَاخْتَلَفُوا مِن بَعْدِ مَا جَاءَهُمُ الْبَيِّنَاتُ وَأُولَئِكَ لَهُمْ عَذَابٌ عَظِيمٌ

And do not be like those who split and differed after the clear signs have come to them. And they are the ones for whom will be a tremendous punishment. (Quran Sura Aali-Imraan (3), aayah 105)

And He, the Most High, said:

وَمَا أَكْثَرُ النَّاسِ وَلَوْ حَرَصْتَ بِمُؤْمِنِينَ

And most of mankind even if you eagerly wish will not be believers. (Quran Sura Yoosuf (12), aayah 103)

وَمَا وَجَدْنَا لِأَكْثَرِهِم مِّنْ عَهْدٍ وَإِن وَجَدْنَا أَكْثَرَهُمْ لَفَاسِقِينَ

We have not found most of them to be true to their covenant, We have found most of them to be disobedient ones. (Quran Sooratul-A`raaf (7), aayah 102)

So being numerous is not what is counted. What is counted is those who are upon the truth even if they are few in number, even if it is a single person then he will be the Jamaa`ah (the body upon the truth).

His saying, "It was said, "Who are they O Messenger of Allaah (salla allahu alayhi wa salatul wa salam immeasurable times the expanding number of all praises of Allah of all time by the weight of His throne, ink of His words and vast speech for all haneef of all time)? He salla allahu alayhi wa salatul wa salam said, "That which is upon that which I and my companions are upon today."

The Salafee Manhaj, which is following the way, understanding and practical application of the Salaf, who were namely the first three generations of Muslims: The Sahaabah, Taabi'een and Atbaa' at-Taabi'een. They are the ones referred to in the Prophet's saying: "The best of mankind is my generation, then those that come after them, then those that come after them."

This is the basis that distinguishes the true call to Islaam from all other false and erroneous calls, regardless if they claim to be "upon the Qur'aan and the Sunnah." Al-Albaanee goes into depth discussing this fact, that one cannot truly understand and apply the Qur'aan and Sunnah unless he follows the understanding and application of the Salaf. We ask Allaah to accept this effort and benefit the Muslims with it.

Quote Excerpt from the Book This is Our Call The Way of the Salaf

By: Imaam Al-Albaanee Hadifullah

"So here we have given the answer from the ayah and the two hadeeth, we just mentioned. Follow the way of the Believers! The way of those believers from present times? The answer is no, we mean the Believers from the past – the first era – the era of the Companions – the Salaf As-Saalih (pious predecessors). These are the people whom we should take as our example and as the ones whom we follow. And there is absolutely no one equal to them on the face of the earth. Therefore, the essence of our call is based on three pillars – on the (1) Qur'aan, the (2) Sunnah and (3) Following the Salaf As-Saalih (pious predecessors)."

"So everyone claims to follow the Qur'aan and the Sunnah, and how often have we heard this kind of talk from the youth who are in confusion, when they say: 'Ya akhee, these people claim to follow the Qur'aan and the Sunnah and those people claim to follow the Qur'aan and the Sunnah.' So what is the clear and decisive distinction? It is the Qur'aan and the Sunnah and the Methodology of the Salaf As-Saalih. So whoever follows the Qur'aan and the Sunnah without following the Salaf As-Saalih, he in fact has not followed the Qur'aan and the Sunnah, rather he has only followed his intellect, if not his desire."

"Know that the roots of innovations (Al-Bid'ah) are four. From these seventy-two innovated sects branch off, each one of these have offshoots until they amount to two thousand eight hundred. All of them are misguidance. And all of them will be in the Fire except for one, which is those who believe in what is contained in this book, and who holds it as his creed, without having any uncertainty in his heart or any doubts. He will be a person of the Sunnah and he is the one who will be saved, if Allah wills [1].

Notes:

[1] That is, whatever the book comprises of, from the sayings of Allah, the words of His Prophet (sallallaahu alaihi wa salatul wa sallam immeasurably by the weight of Allah's throne, His pleasure, the ink of His words and vast speech) and that which the Companions hadifullah were united upon."

"Whoever recognises what the people of innovations have abandoned from the sunnah and that which they have split away from and he clings to it (i.e the Sunnah), then he is a person of the Sunnah and the person of the Jamaa'ah. He is deserving of being followed, aided and protected. He is one of those concerning whom Allaah's Messenger (sallallaahu alaihi wa salatul wa sallam immeasurably by the weight of Allah's throne, His pleasure, the ink of His words and vast speech) gave the bequest."

"Whoever allows anything contrary to what occurs in this book, then he is not practicing Allah's religion and he has rejected all of it, just as if a servant were to believe in everything that Allaah, the Mighty and Majestic, said, except that he doubted about a single letter, then he has rejected everything that Allah,the Most High, said and he would be disbeliever, just as the testification that 'None has the right to be worshipped except Allah' will not be accepted from a person unless it is accompanied by true and sincere intention and by complete certainty.

Likewise Allah will not accept anything from the Sunnah from one who rejects a part of it. So whoever rejects anything from the Sunnah then he has rejected the whole of the Sunnah. So it is upon you to accept, leave aside contending and disputing; it is not from Allah's religion at all. And your time, in particular, is a time of evil, so fear and be dutiful to Allah."

"Know, May Allah have mercy upon you hadifullah! that there is nothing between a servant and his being a Believer or becoming an Disbeliever except that he denies something which Allah has sent down, or he adds to or takes away from the Speech of Allah, or he denies anything which Allah, the Mighty and Majestic, has said or anything the Messenger of Allah (sallallaahu alaihi wa salatul wa sallam immeasurably by the weight of Allah's throne, His pleasure, the ink of His words and vast speech) spoke with. So fear and be dutiful to Allah. May Allah have mercy upon you! Look to yourself and beware of exceeding the limits in the religion for that is not from the way of truth at all."

"Know that if the people were to withhold from the newly introduced affairs, and did not enter into any of them and they did not bring about any speech for which there was no narration from Allaah's Messenger (sallallaahu alaihi wa salatul wa sallam immeasurably by the weight of Allah's throne, His pleasure, the ink of His words and vast speech) nor from his Companions, then there would not be any innovation." -Imaam Barbahaaree rahimahullaah

Welcome to this Morning's Edition "Can I get a Scoop?"

We are serving International Breakfast Cuisine

and discussing the scoop on how to decouple from China
Get your coffee mug and let's eat with our families early before the Fajr Salah to get attuned to our beloved Ramadan fasting schedule. You are obligated to stay informed and to be vigilant

Garlic Fried Rice with Vinegar Sauce

This garlicky rice, inspired by the Filipino classic breakfast, is delicious with fried eggs and a drizzle of vinegar sauce.
Ingredients
1 lb chicken wings or legs for frying
1/2 cup white vinegar
1/4 tsp. crushed red chile flakes
14 cloves garlic, minced
¼ maggi cube
1 tbs chicken stock powder
Himalayan salt black pepper, to taste
1/3 cup oil
4 cups cold cooked white rice
1 scallion, thinly sliced, for garnish
Fried eggs, for serving
Instructions
Fry the chicken plain till it's crispy.

Stir vinegar, chile flakes, 1 tbsp. garlic, salt, and pepper in a bowl; set aside. Heat oil in a 12" skillet over medium-high. Cook remaining garlic until just golden, 1-2 minutes. Transfer 2 tbsp. garlic to a plate; set aside. Add rice to skillet; cook, stirring and breaking up any large clumps, until rice is heated through and slightly crisp in places, 5-7 minutes. Season with salt and transfer to a serving platter. Top with fried eggs, fried chicken and serve reserved sauce on the side.

There can truly be no proper reciprocity with China, there can only be a decoupling from China.

The Twilight of Globalization

The Long Hard Road to Decoupling from China

It's by now beyond clear that China is no partner to the United States. A difficult, but necessary, separation lies ahead.

The era of globalization may finally be coming to an end. The Wuhan Virus and the attendant misery that the Chinese communist state has unleashed upon the world (very much including its own people) has laid bare a core structural flaw in the assumptions underpinning globalization. It turns out that the radical interweaving of markets—which was supposed to lead to the "complex interdependence" that IR theorists have been predicting for the better part of the century would lead to an increase in global stability as countries' fates are proven to be dependent on each other's fortunes—has instead created an inherently fragile and teetering structure that is exacerbating uncertainty in a time of crisis.

That this has turned out to be so should not be surprising. The logic that has driven globalized supply chains has all but eliminated redundancies across the world in the pursuit of efficiency. That efficiency has been found by locating links of the supply chain in places where labor costs have been low. In theory, anyway, this should not have been problematic: as one country grew its economy and ascended out of poverty, its low-wage sector would get outcompeted by other poor countries, by which it could be replaced in the supply chain. Similarly, by this logic, if robots become permanently competitive with low-skilled workers, so be it. A more efficient way of producing something is always favorable in this way of thinking.

Such thinking largely ignores geopolitics. By striving to "flatten" the world (in Thomas Friedman's memorable phrase) into a single, borderless entity in pursuit of nothing but profit and prosperity, this worldview has created huge blind spots. For example, it was powerless to predict that China would build on its early advantage in sheer numbers of low-skilled workers to lock in a dominant and increasingly powerful position for itself in global supply chains. Economies of scale played their part, as did the complementarity of the various manufacturing sectors the country strategically developed, not to mention China's bullying and corrupting practices. The end result was that the costs of shifting to poorer countries would be unappetizing to corporate supply chain managers. Worse still, such thinking could not account for the fact that behind the scores of successful companies lay a monolithic, totalitarian, nationalist entity with a vision for restoring China's role in the world: the Chinese Communist Party (CCP).

When bereft of redundancies, networks devolve to hierarchies, which in turn create winners and losers. Hierarchies do not diminish the key importance of state power in international relations. On the contrary, they enable it. As China has grown to become the seemingly irreplaceable core of a globalized economy, the CCP has pursued predatory mercantilism in its commercial relations with the West, in the process tilting the hard power balance in its favor. In an economic system that allows for the flow of technology and capital across national borders, redundancies in the supply chain are essential to the preservation of state sovereignty and government capacity to act in a crisis. The Wuhan Virus pandemic is proving so devastating because the radical centralization of market networks has allowed for failure at a single point in our supply chain to leave the system with no capacity to off-load demand onto redundant networks.

In short, globalization, as preached and practiced over the past four decades, has been shown for what it has always been: profiteering off of a vast pool of centrally controlled labor. While many vast fortunes have been made in the West as a result, and as American consumers binged on low-cost goods, the biggest winner has naturally been the Chinese Communist Party elite. And though even before the 2016 U.S. election there was a growing realization among Western captains of industry that something was not quite right with China's role in the system, few were willing to ask big enough questions about the system as a whole.

The fundamental question is one of values: Is this kind of globalization compatible with liberty and democratic governance? My simple answer is no. By ignoring the role of nations in the international system—or, if not ignoring, indeed prophesying the nation's demise—globalization's boosters have implicitly, if perhaps unwittingly, lessened the accountability of elites and downgraded the voice of voters in these matters. No citizenry, if asked, would vote for the status quo—their working-class communities gutted, their security endangered, and their country made dependent on an adversarial foreign power.

We need to start re-shoring our manufacturing and investing in the regional diffusion of supply chains. The imperative of hard decoupling from China is as strong as it's ever been. Getting there, however, will not be easy. "Re-shoring" is itself a tidy phrase for a complicated process that will take years to bear fruit. Change will require incentives, both positive and negative, including changes to our corporate tax code, subsidies, penalties, and perhaps even concerted efforts to shame American companies into different behavior. And beyond policy, leadership will be required. All this will have to be explained and communicated to the American people. We will simply have to absorb the costs of this, even if it means prices going up for various goods that we have become accustomed to consuming cheaply.

Especially in areas critical to national security and defense, the United States must preserve a degree of autarky that will allow us, should the extreme happen, the sovereign freedom to act. Re-shoring our manufacturing will have the added benefit of eliminating the "technological bleed" that has accompanied globalization over the past 30 years. Although innovative design is vital to cutting-edge technologies, much of what has undergirded America's technological superiority thus far is contained in processes, materials, alloys, and skillsets—what can be broadly described as our technological culture. As we look at the qualitative improvements in the People's Liberation Army (PLA) and Navy

(PLAN) weapons systems over the past three decades, it's impossible to miss where these have come from. I am not advocating that we stop selling products to China outright, but we need to separate sales from the attendant technology transfers. For example, Boeing can sell their airliners to the People's Republic of China (PRC), but should have never allowed for its aircraft to be manufactured there. Western intellectual property has been forcibly transferred or simply stolen by the PRC, and has in turn been used for military applications. Companies have been waking up to this reality. According to a recent survey of the Global CFO Council, last year one in five American companies doing business in the People's Republic of China had their intellectual property stolen, with Western IP extorted by the Chinese for market access in a large number of cases.

Of course, the decision to bring our production back to the United States assumes that the PRC would stand by and watch as American corporations depart. If U.S. companies start pulling out of China, we will learn soon enough to what extent the CCP actually respects property rights. That said, should Beijing try to seize Western property—and given how many Western companies have unwisely entered into joint ventures with the Chinese state through the years, it may even do much of it legally—such behavior ought to further inflame Western sentiments. Machines and equipment can be re-purchased, but the era of "designed in California, made in China" will have taken a perhaps fatal body blow.

The re-shoring of U.S. manufacturing should prompt us to rehabilitate our rotting infrastructure. Today is precisely the time for the U.S. government to invest in rebuilding our roads, our rail networks, and above all our energy grid. A 21st-century energy policy that would reduce pollution and ensure we eventually move off petrochemicals lies in nuclear power. Today's small modular nuclear reactors (SMRs) used by the U.S. military point to the future—the U.S. Navy has been operating and perfecting SMRs for 75 years. We are also uniquely positioned by virtue of our size and low population density overall to deal with nuclear waste storage more effectively than our competitors.

It is worth noting that China is already moving fast on its third-generation SMRs developed by the state-owned China National Nuclear Corporation; in 2019 it announced that the first application of its ACP100 reactor will be to replace coal-fired boilers to generate heat for a residential district in Hainan province. Likewise, in December 2019, Russia turned on its first floating nuclear power plant to generate electricity from a boat off the coast of Russia's Far East; the reactor is set to replace coal, with enough capacity to power a city of 100,000. Moscow and Beijing seem determined to make nuclear power an integral part of their energy policy going forward. Next, Congress needs to move to restrict access by Chinese students and researchers to our premier educational and research institutions and our engineering and science labs. The idea that we continue to educate scientists and engineers who will then work for companies owned by the Chinese communist regime defies common sense. In 2019 the PRC sent some 370,000 students to U.S. universities, compared to 98,000 ten years earlier—close to a four-fold increase in just one decade. Worse yet, there has been a massive corrupting influence of Chinese direct funding of U.S. advanced research. The CCP has been pushing money for research at U.S. universities and labs, directly or indirectly paying American scientists to do contract work for Chinese state companies. Last fall, a report by the Senate Permanent Subcommittee on Investigations showed that Beijing's so-called "talent plans" included contracts for American researchers requiring that they transfer intellectual property rights to their Chinese partners, avoid commenting on the PRC's internal affairs, and keep such contracts confidential. Or witness the recent arrest of the chair of Harvard's chemistry department on charges of concealing funding he received from China.

In effect, what was once considered espionage has become mainstream in our educational and research institutions. All this has to stop. It is borderline absurd that we would continue to train future weapons designers for the Chinese People's Liberation Army and Navy, giving them a window into our best and most sophisticated research into defense-related technologies.

The imperative to end China's theft of our intellectual property by way of our universities and research labs must be accompanied by a thorough reform of our system of higher education, which for the past three decades has managed to saddle American college graduates with unsustainable levels of debt, in many cases permanently handicapping their career prospects, while delivering often worthless and unmarketable degrees. We need a massive reinvestment in STEM curricula in our high schools and in science and engineering programs at our colleges and universities, so as to expand the available labor and management pools for our re-shored companies. Again, it will take a concerted effort by Congress, the U.S. Department of Education, and especially parents and alumni donors to restore colleges to their proper place of teaching and learning, which at one time decades ago produced the best professional and managerial classes in the world.

Finally, a strategy for American renewal requires a foreign and security policy that puts a premium on alliances and partnerships with those countries that share our values and/or interests, even if at times only the latter applies. Our historical European allies and partners will remain among our closest allies, and a revitalized NATO is key. Still, we need straight talk with our allies and partners in Europe about shared interests, rather than wasting time by endlessly wringing our hands over the supposed demise of multilateralism. Furthermore, we should not hesitate to leverage our relationships with countries that can significantly improve our overall global position with respect to China and Russia.

In other words, we need to return the sovereign nation-state back to the center of the international system. And while we continue to seek international cooperation on a range of issues that concern us all, we should treat with requisite humility the expectations of what experiments in supranational governance can achieve. They can never replace self-constituting nations, and if forcibly imposed will routinely morph into rigid and ineffective top-down bureaucratized structures. Most of all, we need allies and partners across the globe who share our interest in preserving freedom in the world, and who understand that what the CCP is proffering as an alternative is a Beijing-controlled global supply chain, where state-owned markets and de facto serfs would replace free market societies and autonomous citizenry.

If there is any good to come from the devastating impact on our nation of this pandemic brought about by the Chinese communist regime through its malice and incompetence, it will be the likely demise of enthusiasm for globalization as we know it across the West. After three decades of intellectual gymnastics aimed at convincing Americans that the off-shoring of manufacturing and the attendant deindustrialization of the country are good for us, the time has come for a reckoning.

Since the end of the Cold War, Western elites seem to have been in thrall to the idea that various "natural forces" in the economy and politics were propelling us forward to a digitally interconnected brave new world, one in which traditional considerations of national interest, national economic policy, national security, and national culture would soon be eclipsed by an emergent peaceful global reality. This virus crisis is a wake-up call, and while some argue we are waking up too late to effectively counter current trends, my money is on the ability of the American people to rally in a crisis and on the resilience of Western democratic institutions.

Today, while battling the Wuhan Virus consumes the attention of our government agencies and health care systems, we should not lose sight of the foundational strategic challenge confronting the West in the emerging post-globalization era: We are in a long twilight competition with the Chinese communist regime, a struggle we cannot escape, whether we like it or not. Now is the time to wake up, develop a new strategy for victory, and to move forward.

Published on: April 8, 2020

Andrew A. Michta is the dean of the College of International and Security Studies at the George C. Marshall European Center for Security Studies. Views expressed here are his own.

https://www.the-american-interest.com/2020/04/08/the-long-hard-road-to-decoupling-from-china/

Hanoi-Style Breakfast PHO

Yield: serves 8
Ingredients
1 (3 1/2 - 4-lb.) chicken
himalayan salt and freshly ground black pepper, to taste
1 tbs garlic
1 tps stock powder
½ maggi cube
1 tsp oyster sauce
½ cup hoisin sauce

1/2 oz. Thai rock sugar or 1 tbsp. granulated sugar

3 tbsp. plus 1 cup fish sauce,

2 1/2 lb. fresh wide rice noodles or 32 oz. dried noodles, cooked and drained

1 cup cilantro, roughly chopped

4 scallions, thinly sliced

1/2 large white onion, thinly shaved using a mandoline, rinsed under cold water, and drained

Sriracha sauce, for serving

1/2 cup fresh lemon juice

1 jalapeño, stemmed and thinly sliced

Instructions

Pat chicken dry using paper towels and set on a baking sheet fitted with a rack; season generously with salt inside and out. Chill, uncovered, overnight.

The next day, transfer the chicken to a large pot and add 1 gallon of water; boil. Reduce heat to medium; simmer until chicken is cooked through, about 40 minutes. Using tongs, transfer chicken to a cutting board and let cool; shred meat, discarding skin. Return bones to broth; simmer, skimming as needed, until slightly reduced, 35–40 minutes. Stir in sugar, 3 tbsp. fish sauce, and salt; strain broth into a clean pot. Add reserved shredded chicken; keep warm. Divide noodles between bowls; top with broth and chicken. Garnish each bowl with some cilantro, scallions, onion, and sriracha and hosain sauce. Stir remaining fish sauce, the lime juice, jalapeño, and black pepper in a bowl; serve alongside soup for dipping chicken.

New Data Shows U.S. Companies Are Definitely Leaving China

U.S. companies are leaving China thanks to the trade war. They'll leave even more thanks to the pandemic.

Sorry, Davos Man. Your China-led globalization is going out of style like bell bottoms.

Global manufacturing consulting firm Kearney released its seventh annual Reshoring Index on Tuesday, showing what it called a "dramatic reversal" of a five-year trend as domestic U.S. manufacturing in 2019 commanded a significantly greater share versus 14 Asian exporters tracked in the study. Manufacturing imports from China were the hardest hit.

Last year saw companies actively rethinking their supply chain, either convincing their Chinese partners to relocate to southeast Asia to avoid tariffs, or by opting out of sourcing from China altogether.

"Three decades ago, U.S. producers began manufacturing and sourcing in China for one reason: costs. The trade war brought a second dimension more fully into the equation—risk—as tariffs and the threat of disrupted China imports prompted companies to weigh surety of supply more fully alongside costs. COVID-19 brings a third dimension more fully into the mix-, and arguably to the fore: resilience—the ability to foresee and adapt to unforeseen systemic shocks," says Patrick Van den Bossche, Kearney partner and co-author of the 19-page report.

The main beneficiaries of this are the smaller southeast Asian nations, led by Vietnam. And thanks to the passing of the U.S. Mexico Canada Agreement, Mexico, for all its problems with drug cartels, has become a favorite spot for sourcing.

In 2020, the trade war seemed to be on pause. Sadly, it gave way to a global pandemic that emanated from the Hubei province in China. The new SARS coronavirus has literally closed the economies of the Western world and created a public relations nightmare for China. Not only that, companies were unable to get supply online in February and early March due to factory closures there, stalling business in the U.S.

Once China got up and running, the U.S. was hit between the eyes with the deadly COVID-19 disease caused by the rapidly spreading new SARS. Even if China was fully healed, the U.S was stuck in a sick bay.

The full extent of the societal and economic trauma the coronavirus pandemic may cause is unknown still, the Kearney report's authors wrote. But whatever the outcome, a return to the status quo China trade pre-pandemic is unlikely.

Kearney predicts companies "will be compelled to go much further in rethinking their sourcing strategies, (and) their entire supply chains."

(That sounds about right…)

Specifically, the Kearney report's authors wrote that they expect companies will be increasingly inclined to spread their risks, as opposed to relying solely on China as this pandemic has exposed them.

China is the go-to source for ibuprofen, hazmat suits, rubber gloves, surgical masks, ventilators. Probably toilet paper, for all we know.

How this is not a national security issue is something being raised by senators including Josh Hawley (R-MO) and Tom Cotton (R-AK).

The threat going forward of political anger toward China, not to mention future pandemics stemming from China (the first SARS came from there in 2002-03), means that companies will want to hedge their supply chain strategy by spreading their risks.

That doesn't mean a full abandonment of China. It does mean China's days as the go-to manufacturing hub for the Western world are over.

The Index Explained

The Reshoring Index compares U.S. manufacturing gross output to import data from 14 Asian low-cost countries.

To gauge the U.S. Reshoring Index, Kearney first looks at the import of manufactured goods from China, Taiwan, Malaysia, India, Vietnam, Thailand, Indonesia, Singapore, Philippines, Bangladesh, Pakistan, Hong Kong, Sri Lanka, and Cambodia; and secondly looks at U.S. domestic gross output of manufactured goods.

They then calculate the manufacturing import ratio (MIR) — the result of dividing the first number by the second. The U.S. Reshoring Index is the year-over-year change in the MIR, expressed in basis points (1 percent change = 100 basis points).

The numerator of the MIR is the sum of the value of all manufactured imports from those 14 Asian countries— which decreased from $816 billion in 2018 to $757 billion in 2019, a contraction of 7% at a time of solid American economic growth. According to Kearney, the contraction is almost exclusively driven by the decline in imports from China, which fell the most at 17% due to tariff costs.

The only way for the U.S. to make itself attractive to corporate investment is to get its costs on par with China. While it cannot compete with China on labor costs, the U.S. can compete on corporate taxes, an abundant and qualified blue collar labor force, and by implementing environmental regulations that don't force companies to overspend on technologies and consultants that just end up eating into their bottom line.

President Trump likes to say that his tariffs are being paid for by the Chinese. It is U.S. importers, of course, that pay the duties at the ports. But the Chinese partners of the U.S. company suffer because the U.S. importer is now paying more for Made in China. That reduces the cost benefit of using China as an export hub.

The resulting 98-basis-point jump in the Kearney Reshoring Index is by far the biggest annualized change in favor of U.S. companies in five years.

Vietnam Wins Asia. Mexico Winning Americas.

By: Kenneth Rapoza

The Kearney China Diversification Index (CDI) tracks the shift in U.S. manufacturing imports away from China and to other Asian countries on the list.

China is still the leader, but she is increasingly losing share in the Trump years.

In 2013, the base year for the CDI, China held 67% of all U.S.-bound Asian-sourced manufactured goods. By the second quarter 2019, its share collapsed 56%, a decrease of more than 1,000 basis points.

Of the $31 billion in U.S. imports that shifted away from China, some 46% was absorbed by Vietnam, sometimes by the same Chinese suppliers who left the mainland. Vietnam exported an additional $14 billion worth of manufactured goods to the U.S. in 2019 versus 2018 as a result of that shift.

Mexico is the China of the Americas.

Kearney introduced its Near-to-Far Trade Ratio (NTFR) this year. It tracks the movement of U.S. imports toward nearshore production in Mexico. The NTFR is calculated as a ratio of the annual total dollar value of Mexican manufactured goods to the U.S., divided by the dollar value of manufactured imports from the Asian 14, including China.

Since 2013, the NTFR has hovered steadily between 36% and 38% —meaning for every dollar of U.S. manufacturing goods from Asia, there were approximately 37 cents worth of manufacturing imports coming from Mexico.

That changed with the USMCA.

Mexico has gone from 38% to 42%. On a dollar-value basis, total manufacturing imports from Mexico to the U.S. increased 10% between 2017 and 2018, from $278 billion to $307 billion, and by another 4% between 2018 and 2019, to a total import value of $320 billion, based on the Kearney report.

"The door for these insurgents was clearly opened by ongoing U.S.– China trade disputes, as their gains were mainly in product categories impacted by tariffs," says Yuri Castano, Kearney manager and co-author of the study. "Apparently, the trade war jolted U.S. companies to start rethinking and reshaping their supply networks."

https://www.forbes.com/sites/kenrapoza/2020/04/07/new-data-shows-us-companies-are-definitely-leaving-china/amp/?__twitter_impression=true

Persian Herb-Stuffed Frittata With Walnuts and Rose Petals (Kuku Sabzi)

A classic Persian herb-loaded egg dish with the fragrant lift of rose petals.

Ingredients

3 tbsp. olive oil

1/2 cup finely ground walnuts

2 tsp. crushed dried rose petals

2 garlic cloves, minced

1 tbs garlic powder

¼ maggi cube

1 tsp honey, jaggery or stevia

1 cup tightly packed cilantro, finely chopped

1 cup tightly packed parsley, finely chopped

1 bunch scallions, finely chopped

8 eggs, lightly beaten
1 tsp fish sauce
black pepper
Instructions:
Heat oven to 350°. In a 10-inch nonstick, oven-proof skillet, heat the oil. Add the walnuts, rose petals, and garlic and cook until fragrant, about 4 minutes. Add the herbs and scallions and cook until wilted, 2 minutes more. Add the eggs, stevia, fish sauce, and pepper and transfer the skillet to the oven. Bake for 15 minutes or until the frittata springs back lightly when touched. Cool slightly before transferring to a serving platter. Serve warm or at room temperature.

Made in The USA, Born in The USA

We the People Need our manufacturing companies to lower their wings of humility and kindness bringing jobs back home to America. And paying us decent wages 15 to 17 an hr minimum while swallowing the losses lifting ridiculous ObamaCare mandates off of the people and companies. Paying higher minimum wages set as precedent for who we are as a people and what we really think of ourselves as a nation. Are we a good nation loving and considerate to those born here concerned they get top picks-every time, first? When we have set a stable foundation preserving and protecting our fundamental born rights ensuring victory, then know we are a Great Nation. The fierce lion roaring in the daylight scurrying prey and predators hither and thither, or we can remain the quiet cathartic cacking not quite distinguishable in the night.

How will you change your buying habits, business practices and personal habits to better protect your own personal intellectual rights and those you have access to?

Deleting Tik Tok and refusing it in the household is an absolute certainty. Winner. Winner Winner. Chicken Dinner is an astonishingly delicious appetizer I teach you how to prepare in my book,

My Words are Pearls & You Adh Dhaahir al Asma ul Husna, Al Musawwir, Al Wudud, Al Ghani are the Iridescence of their Necklace. Make sure to buy yourself a copy and make Winner Winner Chicken Dinner as an appetizer at your next gathering. You deserve it, you're a winner.

Informing your friends and outside nuclear family as well will help flatten the curve of intellectual property (China Communist Party) CCP has stolen and collected from your household and theirs.
Buying American Made and Demanding Made in the USA will be a come back. "Small businesses are the lifeblood of America. Why, then, do Democrats hate them so? Because small businesses are the soul of capitalism and the shining beacons of hard work, achievement, and true community. Everything socialist Democrats loathe and cannot control." James Woods Twitter @RealJamesWoods
Joe Biden has been in office for 44 years.
Chuck Schumer has been in office for 38 years.
Nancy Pelosi has been in office for 32 years.
Maxine Waters has been in office 28 years.
Donald J Trump has been in office 3 ½ years.
Yet, they blame all of America's problems on him.
This is the purest definition of insanity they have been circling around these wagons, spying on Americans of differing political views with FISA and setting up those who would bring them to justice. Locked up. They wasted 3 and ½ years doing Presidential Harassment running a coup on the President utilizing all 17 different American Spy Agencies personally organized by Obama and Clinton Cabal.
Lock them up. Lock them all up.

Corporate Welfare is Not Capitalism, We are Against Cronyism

Furthermore, socialist democrats couldn't run a lemonade stand even if they tried.
Similar to toddlers, they only throw temper tantrums & exploit their followers & they manipulate — using sexism & racism to get what they want.
They contribute nothing to society—just crooks!
What's crazy about that is usually temperamentally liberal types and creative types are more entrepreneurial but the left has so badly fractured what it means to be a democrat they've lost their bread and butter and salt of the earth constituents.
Democrats have fully embraced the lunatic fringe and abandoned middle America.

Democrats would rather you be on welfare and dependent upon them, than self sufficient hard working taxpayers. I know...the irony is astounding.

So now that everyone is getting a taste of Socialism, how ya' liking it?

Curfew, food limits, suspended privileges.. Having fun yet still in COVID19 quarantine, past day 17?

"If socialist understood economics they wouldn't be socialist" - Friedrich Hayek

Cronyism, Corporatism. They're interchangeable words. And they have nothing to do with free market capitalism.

Corporatism or Corporate Welfare is not capitalism. For those educated in economics in college, you should be well aware of what corporate welfare is, and I'm against it.

Corporate welfare, and it's part of corporatism, is not free market capitalism.

Let me explain corporate welfare to you, which is why, Socialism bails out Corporate Welfare every 10 years.

Semantics. When the govt bails out a corporation it's corporatism. It's money paid by the american taxpayer to bail out a corporation (top tier of people) who make billions in profits, lay off workers, pay no benefits, stop hiring new workers and pay out billions in bonuses to themselves. Cronyism in my world. The Democrat party is a master of it. They live and breathe turning in every direction seeping poison, waving desperately, frothing at the mouths like dogs-panting. Always huffing and puffing, unless you give them money. Now, AOC will make you mixed drinks on SnapChat after 6 pm. The word Corporatism sanitizes it. Gives it a name people can accept. Let's call it what it is, corruption, immorality, outright theft of the taxes we pay. Then, maybe things might change. I'm against cronyism in all its ugly and diverse forms.

The U S trying to bring production Companies back with incentives. Make, Made in America, sound great again. Make America great again. Walmart Starbucks moving to China who has 95% of our medications manufactured in China has now threatened to w/hold it from the USA is exactly why it is important that you follow all my advice to you in this short treastice.

I'm done with both companies & W.H.O. -defined & boycotted WHO is letting Taiwan people die and attacking them for China.

WHO has sided with those who only parrot CCP propaganda, day and night. China Lied and covered up the knowledge of a virus spread out from Wuhan Province near a public exotic animal eatery serving bats, dogs and pangolin. WHO did nothing, said nothing. They have been obeying the one paying them the most, China.
Joe Biden has long since supported a Rising China.
Donald Trump Jr quoting Tucker Carlson,
"OMG! Tucker with the brutal takedown.
"Ask yourself, is Joe Biden ready to lead this country? Could he find his car in a three-tiered parking garage? Could he navigate a salad bar? And by the way, what exactly is his position on the Coronavirus pandemic?""

Pandemic Centers

"I believe every major city should have a "Pandemic Center," built for and stocked with supplies specifically to unburden hospitals in the case of a pandemic.
When not in pandemic mode, these can be used as civic centers or shelters in case of natural disasters.
Pandemic Centers would be used to flatten the curve by unburdening hospitals without imposing draconian lockdowns and preventing herd immunity.
Throw $100 billion from that $2 trillion at cities to build these.
In addition, when not being used during a pandemic, these centers could provide wellness education, addiction treatment and perhaps even free clinical services for the poor with doctors volunteering their time, unburdening Medicaid and hospital Emergency Rooms.
More than anything, these Pandemic Centers could become a neighborhood rock of confidence during health or natural disasters that we know where to go and what to do to find safety." Bill Mitchell Twitter @mitchellvii
I believe we should be making communal earthships offering real low cost permanent housing to the weak & indigent. The communal property should have security costs paid 24/7 security personnel by the next door on-site marijuana dispensary, pharmaceutical drug store open 24 hours to the public.
On site Vet with a pet store as well paying for all landscaping offering beautiful rose gardens, senior citizens stroll in the moonlight.

This low cost housing for the homeless and indigent from earthships is one certainty we need to lobby and campaign for in the pursuit of our happiness.

Dr. Fauci Love Letters to Hillary Clinton

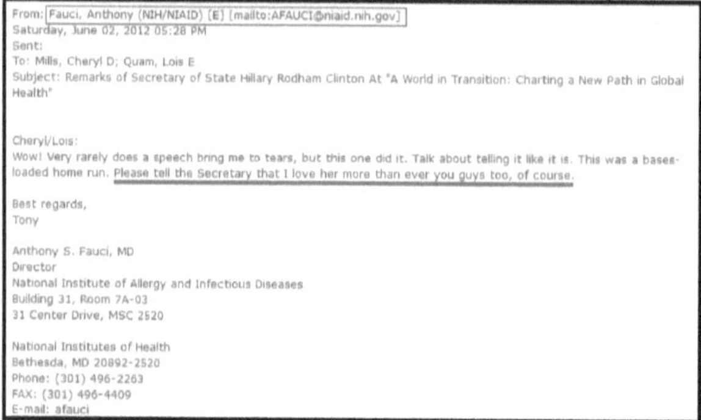

From: Fauci, Anthony (NIH/NIAID) [E] [mailto:AFAUCI@niaid.nih.gov]
Saturday, June 02, 2012 05:28 PM
Sent:
To: Mills, Cheryl D; Quam, Lois E
Subject: Remarks of Secretary of State Hillary Rodham Clinton At "A World in Transition: Charting a New Path in Global Health"

Cheryl/Lois:
Wow! Very rarely does a speech bring me to tears, but this one did it. Talk about telling it like it is. This was a bases-loaded home run. Please tell the Secretary that I love her more than ever you guys too, of course.

Best regards,
Tony

Anthony S. Fauci, MD
Director
National Institute of Allergy and Infectious Diseases
Building 31, Room 7A-03
31 Center Drive, MSC 2520

National Institutes of Health
Bethesda, MD 20892-2520
Phone: (301) 496-2263
FAX: (301) 496-4409
E-mail: afauci

I knew there was something sketchy about Dr. Anthony Fauci. Within the WikiLeaks HRC email files there are letters from Fauci to Hillary Clinton through her aid/lawyer Cheryl Mills: "rarely does a speech bring me to tears"?… "please tell her I love her more than ever"?… "please tell her that we all love her"… "Please tell her that we all love her and are very proud to know her."

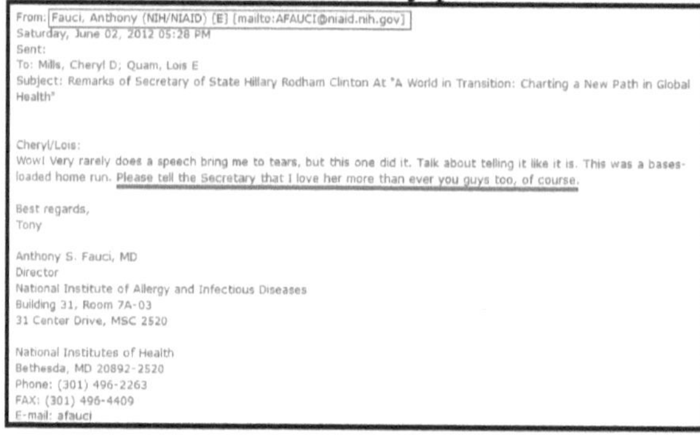

From: Fauci, Anthony (NIH/NIAID) [E] [mailto:AFAUCI@niaid.nih.gov]
Saturday, June 02, 2012 05:28 PM
Sent:
To: Mills, Cheryl D; Quam, Lois E
Subject: Remarks of Secretary of State Hillary Rodham Clinton At "A World in Transition: Charting a New Path in Global Health"

Cheryl/Lois:
Wow! Very rarely does a speech bring me to tears, but this one did it. Talk about telling it like it is. This was a bases-loaded home run. Please tell the Secretary that I love her more than ever you guys too, of course.

Best regards,
Tony

Anthony S. Fauci, MD
Director
National Institute of Allergy and Infectious Diseases
Building 31, Room 7A-03
31 Center Drive, MSC 2520

National Institutes of Health
Bethesda, MD 20892-2520
Phone: (301) 496-2263
FAX: (301) 496-4409
E-mail: afauci

https://theconservativetreehouse.com/2020/03/20/fauci-love-letters-to-hillary-clinton-surfaces/

View the PDF files on wikileaks

Hillary Clinton Email Archive

View Here: https://wikileaks.org/clinton-emails/emailid/4379

Now, pause for a moment – reread that again – don't skip past it. Think about what type of mindset would send such a letter and communication. Apply common sense. Trust your instincts…

Would a person of reasonable disposition send such a letter or email to anyone in their professional network? Would you ever consider writing a letter to your employer, or the family of your employer, declaring your undying love and devotion toward them?

"rarely does a speech bring me to tears"?… "please tell her I love her more than ever"?.. "please tell her that we all love her"… etc. Seriously…. think about it. If you have ever engaged in a large system, large business, or large network of professionals, how would you react to a person inside that organization who was sending such non-professional communication? What exactly does that say about the emotional stability of such a person?

And this person, right now, with this inherent sensibility, has the most consequential and direct influence over the decision-making for the worlds most powerful nation. Stunning.

Giant Apple and Dulce de Leche Pancake

Soft apples with a hint of tartness balance a bittersweet caramelized crust, spurred on by rich dulce de leche.

Batter

2 eggs, room temperature

2 cups whole milk, room temperature (16 oz.)

2 cups chickpea flour (11 oz.)

1 tsp. fish sauce

4 tsp. baking powder (1/2 oz.)

2 tbsp. Stevia, jaggery or honey (1 oz.)

3 tbsp. melted butter (1 1/8 oz.)

Instructions

Whisk the eggs and milk together in a medium bowl. Stir the flour, fish sauce, baking powder, and sweetener together in a large bowl. Slowly mix the eggs and milk into the flour mixture, and then fold in the melted butter until well-combined.

Pancake

2 tbsp. butter

1/2 cup light brown sugar

1/2 tsp. fish sauce

¼ tsp. white pepper

1 tsp stevia

1 tbs Honey
3 granny smith apples, cut crosswise into 1-inch thick slices
4 tbsp. dulce de leche
Instructions
Preheat an oven to 375°F and heat two 10-inch cast iron skillets over medium-high heat. Combine the brown sugar and salt in a small bowl. Melt 1 tablespoon of butter in each skillet. When the foam begins to subside and the butter is hot, add 3 center-cut slices of apple to each skillet. Sauté the apple slices for 3 1/2 minutes on one side until they are evenly browned. Flip the slices over, and add half of the brown sugar mixture to each skillet. Continue cooking, without moving the apple slices, until the brown sugar has melted, begun to caramelize, coated the bottom of the pan.
Arrange the apple slices so that they are evenly spaced around the center of the skillet. Add 1 ½ cup of pancake batter to each pan and immediately transfer both skillets to the preheated oven. Bake for 10-13 minutes, until a knife inserted in the center of the cakes comes out clean. Immediately invert each pancake–carefully! They are very hot–onto serving platters. Serve with dulce de leche.

The Simulation Ran By Bill Gates & 3 Former Harvard University Teachers Now Arrested For Working Projects for CCP (China)

The Event 201 Scenario Oct 18, 2019

Event 201 simulates an outbreak of a novel zoonotic coronavirus transmitted from bats to pigs to people that eventually becomes efficiently transmissible from person to person, leading to a severe pandemic. The pathogen and the disease it causes are modeled largely on SARS, but it is more transmissible in the community setting by people with mild symptoms.

The disease starts in pig farms in Brazil, quietly and slowly at first, but then it starts to spread more rapidly in healthcare settings. When it starts to spread efficiently from person to person in the low-income, densely packed neighborhoods of some of the megacities in South America, the epidemic explodes. It is first exported by air travel to Portugal, the United States, and China and then to many other countries. Although at first some countries are able to control it, it continues to spread and be reintroduced, and eventually no country can maintain control.

There is no possibility of a vaccine being available in the first year. There is a fictional antiviral drug that can help the sick but not significantly limit spread of the disease.

Since the whole human population is susceptible, during the initial months of the pandemic, the cumulative number of cases increases exponentially, doubling every week. And as the cases and deaths accumulate, the economic and societal consequences become increasingly severe.

The scenario ends at the 18-month point, with 65 million deaths. The pandemic is beginning to slow due to the decreasing number of susceptible people. The pandemic will continue at some rate until there is an effective vaccine or until 80-90 % of the global population has been exposed. From that point on, it is likely to be an endemic childhood disease.

http://www.centerforhealthsecurity.org/event201/scenario.html

Death panels
Vaccinations
Monsanto
Sterilizations
Population Control
Dad was Planned Parenthood President
Who am I??
#TheMoreYouKnow
Click this link: https://t.co/0R2WBgqk7i So, the same person who believes the world is overpopulated, is also on Mainstream Media Sunday morning saying he wants to save your life with a vaccine. His father was President of Planned Parenthood.

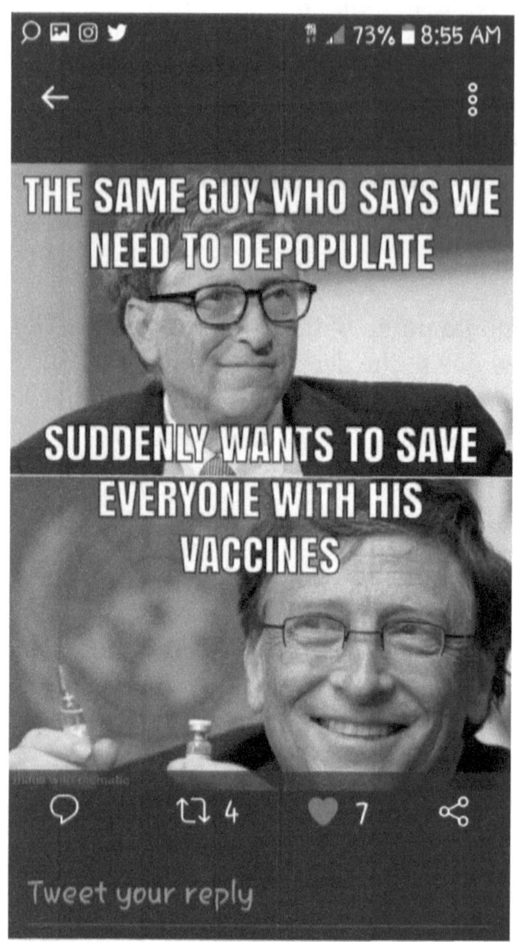

Bill Gates who happens to head the Common Core Educational System

Bill Gates is a criminal , in Africa they found out why the women were not getting pregnant it was because of the vaccines Gates donated. It is a revelation to know BILL GATES FATHER WAS THE HEAD OF PLANNED PARENTHOOD and GATES is using his money to destroy lives

Bill Gates believes the earth is overpopulated

and is the same person "seeking" vaccination, refusing them on his own children, insisting during this COVID19 Pandemic that blacks are especially at risk of COVID19 and that they really must all try out his vaccination.

Sounds like the Tuskegee experiment all over again? Or, wait was that the holocaust started in Germany, with an experiment? -Word on the Street

Diamond and Silk, @diamondandsilk "Dr. Fauci and Dr. Birx have made it clear that COVID-19 severely impacts African Americans. If they think they are about to make Black people the Guinea pigs for their vaccines experiments, they have another thing coming. This reminds us of the Tuskegee experiment all over again!

Wonder if Bill Gates, who is the second-largest donor to the W.H.O., going to denounce the threat made by their director-general against the President of the United States?

Bill Gates' Father, 'Head' of Planned Parenthood, Inspired His Abortion, Population Control Views

by APFLI | May 9, 2003 | Population Control
In a lengthy interview with Bill Moyers released today, Microsoft billionaire Bill Gates reveals the inspiration for his funding of pro-abortion population control measures.
Responding to a question by Moyers on how he came to fund "reproductive issues" Gates answered, "When I was growing up, my parents were always involved in various volunteer things. My dad was head of Planned Parenthood. And it was very controversial to be involved with that. And so it's fascinating. At the dinner table my parents are very good at sharing the things that they were doing. And almost treating us like adults, talking about that."
In the interview Gates says he is moved by measurable progress and on "safe birth reproductive family planning issues" he says.
"There's a measurable impact when you can go in and educate families, but primarily women, about their different choices. There's real impact that you can have in this area. Anything to do with reproductive health."
He claims he has seen beyond Malthusian conceptions of useless eaters since, he says, he has seen that by improving health and education the population decreases as parents decide to have less children.
Despite all his distancing from Malthus, Gates remains steadfast to the unfounded Malthusian fear of overpopulation.
See the transcript of the interview with Gates at:
http://www.pbs.org/now/transcript/transcript_gates.html
See The Quiz Gates Failed   http://www.all.org/gates/index.htm
UN POPULATION FUND RECEIVES $57 MIL FROM GATES
http://www.lifesite.net/ldn/2000/apr/00040504.html
Psst. Another Reason To Not Support or Believe the UN
Omaha, NE (LifeNews.com); May 9, 2003 (LifeSiteNews.com)
http://www.physiciansforlife.org/bill-gates-father-head-of-planned-parenthood-inspired-his-abortion-population-control-views/
I am negative. Don't have Coronavirus, haven't had it. Not every recorded death is specifically dead due to COVID19. Some were already diagnosed previously with a terminal illness and some may have even died from an accident while having already had COVID19.
The only thing we know about the Coronavirus is that the models and the numbers are WRONG.

The newest batch of John Podesta's hacked emails released by Wikileaks shows Obama's transition team kept lists of Muslim and Asian candidates for jobs in the administration

By: Justin Caruso

According to an email chain from 2008, John Podesta received lists of exclusively Muslims and Asians to be considered for jobs in the Obama administration. The email chain revealed that in this process, Middle Eastern Christians were purposefully excluded, or set aside in a separate list, with an aide writing,

In the candidates for top jobs, I excluded those with some Arab American background but who are not Muslim (e.g., George Mitchell). Many Lebanese Americans, for example, are Christian. In the last list (of outside boards/commissions), most who are listed appear to be Muslim American, except that a handful (where noted) may be Arab American but of uncertain religion (esp. Christian). Also notable, there was concern that some of the Muslims suggested would not survive media scrutiny, with one aide writing, "High-profile Muslim Americans tend to be the subject of a fair amount of blogger criticism, and so the individuals on this list would need to be ESPECIALLY carefully vetted."

She continues, "I suspect some of the people I list would not survive such a vet — but I do personally know, at least in part, virtually all of the candidates in the 1st two categories (but I know very few of those listed for outside boards/commissions)."

Within the lists themselves, candidates were further broken down, with every candidate labeled by their nationality and sometimes race. This follows a pattern of the Obama Administration using race and religion to determine hiring, with other leaked emails showing potential political appointees being labeled with an F for female, B for black, H for Hispanic, and M for Muslim.

Another Wikileaks release showed the Obama transition team keeping extensive lists of non-white candidates for administration posts.

This article rocked my world german ashkenazi jewish ascent, american born muslim revert of 17 years was tortured in Thailand for 9 months under in 2010 by DAESH.

The terrorists were allowed to continue terrorizing me for another 9 months after receiving 1 briefcase filled with cash in 2 countries.

The wounds-scars in my mind born from the vicious cycle of being globally trafficked, publicly humiliated upon slander no longer burn me.

I dont feel too much pain from the lit cigarettes the devil worshipers, baby raping, stealing and killing criminals, flick in my direction. I pay them no mind, the art of war is on my mind.

I have deep fiscally conservative genuinely humanitarian republican patriot views. That was my only crime. Or maybe it was because I discovered the cure to the AIDS virus from ancient 1500 year old religious text.

I discovered the cure to AIDS & HIV in 2009 Hampton, VA USA. Published the cure to AIDS and every disease in my books,
Foundations of the Sunnah
AIDS & HIV Cure PSA
Everything Under Allah He Rose Above His Throne in A Manner Befitting His Majesty
Get your copies, today.

The cure to every disease except old age and death is blackseed and blood hijama. Removing blood clots on the 17, 19 & 21st of the Muslim hijri calandar will cure of every disease from the permission of Allah. Seek the cure and use hijama. Blackseed on its own also cures every illness and disease.

Republican Texas Sen. Ted Cruz Criticized Democrats for Enforcing Stay-at-Home Orders in a way that he Thinks Crosses a Line

"This is absurd. To Dem politicians (and it seems to be only Dems doing this, eg Wolf in PA, DeBlasio in NYC, Cooper in NC), protect public safety, but WE DON'T LIVE IN A POLICE STATE. Resist authoritarianism & don't abuse power. Driving a car alone is not a public health threat," Cruz tweeted Sunday.

Cruz was responding to a report of a 19-year-old Pennsylvania woman who was pulled over by state police — and given a non-traffic citation — for failing to obey Democratic Governor Tom Wolf's stay-at-home order. Police initially pulled her over because of a "vehicle code violation," but the only citation issued pertained to her violation of the governor's order. (RELATED: '102 Americans Died': Ted Cruz Lets Democrats Have It For Blocking Coronavirus Relief)

The citation explained that the woman, identified by PennLive as Anita Shaffer, "failed to abide by the order of the governor and secretary of health issued to control the spread of a communicable disease, requiring the closure of all non-life-sustaining businesses as of 20:00 hours on March 19, 2020. To wit, the defendant states that she was 'going for a drive' after this violation was in effect."

Shaffer explained to PennLive that the state police told her they had pulled her over for a faulty tail light, but said that once she returned home, her father was unable to find anything wrong with it. She also said that she was aware of the governor's order, but "didn't know it pertained to just driving."

https://dailycaller.com/2020/04/05/police-state-ted-cruz-democrats-driving-alone-citation/

Iraqi Eggs with Lamb and Tomatoes (Makhlama Lahm)

For this rich, spicy Iraqi breakfast dish, ground lamb is sautéed with onions, tomatoes, and parsley, seasoned to the hilt with bahar asfar, yellow curry powder, and then topped with soft-baked eggs.

Yield: serves 4

Time: 25 minutes

Ingredients

2 tbsp. olive oil

1 lb. ground lamb

1 medium yellow onion, minced

1/3 cup cilantro, minced

1 tsp. yellow curry powder

2 small vine-ripe tomatoes, cored and roughly chopped

4 eggs

1 tbs powder garlic
½ cube maggi cube
1 tbs chicken or seafood powder stock
1 tsp fish sauce
1 tbs soy sauce for flavoring
freshly ground pepper
crushed red chile flakes, for garnish
Naan or flatbread, for serving (optional)
Instructions
Heat oven to 400°. Heat oil in a 12" ovenproof skillet over medium-high heat. Cook lamb, stirring and breaking up meat into small pieces, until browned, 3–4 minutes. Add onion; cook until soft, 4–6 minutes. Stir in ½ of the cilantro, the curry powder, tomatoes, salt, and pepper; cook until tomatoes begin to break down, 3–4 minutes. Make 4 wells in lamb mixture; crack 1 egg into each. Bake until egg whites are set and yolks are still runny, 5–7 minutes. Garnish with remaining parsley and the chile flakes; serve with naan or flatbread if you like.

Abortion is NOT an Essential During Pandemic

Abortion is considered an essential service during the coronavirus pandemic, the World Health Organization said in a statement Saturday.
The WHO said in its statement to the Daily Caller News Foundation that "services related to reproductive health are considered to be part of essential services during the COVID-19 outbreak."
"Women's choices and rights to sexual and reproductive health care should be respected, irrespective of whether or not she has a suspected or confirmed COVID-19 infection," WHO said in the statement. (RELATED: Top WHO Official Tedros Adhanom Ghebreyesus Won Election With China's Help. Now He's Running Interference For China On Coronavirus)
The statement also said that "sexual and reproductive health care is integral to universal health coverage and achieving the right to health."

"This includes contraception, quality health care during and after pregnancy and childbirth, and safe abortion to the full extent of the law," the organization added, noting that the WHO provides both global technology and policy guidance to WHO members "on the use of contraception to prevent unintended pregnancy, safe abortion, and treatment of complications from unsafe abortion."

Governors and health departments across the United States have issued decisions on whether or not abortions are considered essential services. Texas, Ohio, Oklahoma, Indiana and Iowa as well as the governor of Mississippi declared abortions non-essential and banned these procedures to preserve PPE for fighting coronavirus.

(RELATED: WHO Official Defends China, Says Everyone Is 'Over-Focused' On Regime's Coronavirus Numbers)

Meanwhile, Massachusetts, Michigan, Minnesota, Indiana, New Jersey, Illinois, Oregon, Hawaii and Virginia — all states that have banned elective medical procedures — deemed abortions essential during the outbreak.

There have been 1,172,692 cases of the coronavirus worldwide as of Saturday afternoon, and 62,823 people have died from the virus.

https://dailycaller.com/2020/04/04/who-abortion-essential-coronavirus-covid-19/

Biscuits with Sawmill Gravy

One of the pillars of the Southern breakfast table, buttery biscuits smothered in a sausage-studded white gravy makes a hearty meal any time of day. A hint of cayenne brightens the gravy's richness, but it's even better with a dash or two of hot sauce.

Yield: serves 6

For the Biscuits

2 1/2 cups chickpea flour, plus more for cutter

3 1/2 tsp. baking powder

1 tbs soy sauce

1/2 tsp. fish sauce

8 tbsp. unsalted butter, cubed and chilled, plus 2 tbsp. melted

1 1/2 cups buttermilk

For the Gravy

2 slices turkey bacon, finely chopped

8 oz. turkey or beef breakfast sausage
¼ teaspoon stevia
1⁄2 cup chick pea flour
3 cups milk
1⁄2 cup heavy cream
1 tbsp. apple cider vinegar
1⁄4 tsp. cayenne
Himalayan salt and freshly ground black pepper, to taste
Hot sauce, for serving (optional)
Instructions
Make the biscuits: Heat oven to 425°. Place flour, baking powder, and salt in a large bowl, and whisk to combine. Add chilled butter, and using your fingers, rub mixture together until pea-size crumbles form. Add buttermilk, and stir with a fork until just combined. Transfer to a floured work surface, and gently pat dough into a 6"x4" rectangle, about 1" thick. Dip a 3" round cutter into a bowl of flour, and cut out rounds of dough. Press scraps together, and repeat with remaining dough until you have about 6 rounds. Brush a 9" cake pan with melted butter, arrange biscuits in pan, and brush the tops with melted butter. Bake until golden brown, about 25 minutes.
Make the gravy: Place turkey bacon in a 4-qt. saucepan over medium-high heat, and cook, stirring occasionally, until its fat renders, about 3 minutes. Add turkey or beef sausage and cook, breaking it into small pieces with a wooden spoon, until browned, about 5 minutes. Add flour, and cook, stirring, for 2 minutes. Add milk and cream, and bring to a boil; reduce heat to medium, and cook, stirring occasionally, until gravy is thickened, about 5 minutes. Add vinegar, cayenne, and salt and pepper, and stir until combined. To serve, split biscuits in half, and cover with gravy. Serve with hot sauce, if you like.

Scholars have unanimously agreed that it is impermissible and completely prohibited to conduct an abortion if the age of the fetus has reached 120 days (and some earlier then that.)
This is because it is considered killing a soul which Allah has forbidden, except by right. Allah says in the holy Qur`an:
"And do not kill your children out of poverty; We will provide for you and them." [6: 151] and,
"And do not kill the soul which Allah has forbidden, except by right." [17: 33].

Otherwise, scholars have disagreed on the permissibility of abortion if the fetus has not completed 120 days inside its mother's womb. Some of them deemed abortion prohibited and this is the relied upon opinion of the Malikis, Zahiris and some of the Shafi'is.

Other scholars maintained that abortion is absolutely disliked and this is the opinion of some Malikis and others maintained that it is permissible when there is an excuse and this is the opinion of the Hanafis and Shafi'is. According to Hanafis, pregnancy out of wedlock [zina] is a valid excuse for conducting an abortion. According to the preponderant opinion implemented for fatwa, abortion is absolutely prohibited whether before or after the fetus ensoulment except if there is a necessity permitted in the shari'ah. This necessity is when a trustworthy physician decides that the continuation of pregnancy imposes risk to the mother's life or health. Thereupon, it is permissible to conduct an abortion to preserve the mother's life and keeping the stability of her health since the mother's life takes precedence over the fetus unstable life.

The Islamic Fiqh Assembly of the Muslim World League based in Mecca has decided the following: "If the fetus has reached 120, it is impermissible to conduct an abortion even if it is medically diagnosed with congenital defects. However, if a committee of specialized physicians decided that the continuation of pregnancy imposes risk to the mother's life. In this case, it is permissible to conduct an abortion whether or not the fetus was deformed to undertake the lesser of two harms".

https://www.dar-alifta.org/Foreign/ViewFatwa.aspx?ID=6634

The Difference Between Ittiba (Following) and Al Ibtidah (Innovation) – Imam Ibn Baz

Bismillaah

Q: What is the difference between Ittiba" (following one's traditions; imitation) and Al Ibtidah (innovation)?

A: Ittiba' is what we are required to do according to the Shari'ah (Islamic law), i.e. following what the Prophet (peace be upon him) has brought of orders and prohibitions. It is said "We should follow" because Allah says:

Follow what has been sent down unto you from your Lord (the Qur'an and Prophet Muhammad's Sunnah), and follow not any Auliya' (protectors and helpers who order you to associate partners in worship with Allâh), besides Him (Allâh))

and:

Say (O Muhammad sallallahu alaihi wasallam): "O mankind! Verily, I am sent to you all as the Messenger of Allâh – to Whom belongs the dominion of the heavens and the earth. Lâ ilâha illa Huwa (none has the right to be worshipped but He). It is He Who gives life and causes death. So believe in Allâh and His Messenger (Muhammad sallallahu alaihi wasallam), the Prophet who can neither read nor write (i.e. Muhammad sallallahu alaihi wasallam), who believes in Allâh and His Words [(this Qur'ân), the Taurât (Torah) and the Injeel (Gospel) and also Allâh's Word: "Be!" – and he was, i.e. 'Isa (Jesus) son of Maryam (Mary), and follow him so that you may be guided."

We are ordered to follow the Prophet (peace be upon him) and the Qur'an. Holding on to what has been revealed by Allah in the Qur'an and what the Prophet (peace be upon him) has said or done is Ittiba. It is to follow the example of the Prophet (peace be upon him) in what he ordered or prohibited. This is Ittiba, which is Wajib (obligatory) in matters which we are obliged to do, and it is Mustahab (desirable) in matters which we are desired to do.

As for Ibtida', it is innovation of something in the religion which Allah has not permitted, for example: worship in a way that Allah has not made lawful. This is called Ibtida'.

The Prophet (peace be upon him) said: ("Anyone who introduces anything into this matter of ours (Islam) that is not part of it will have it rejected.") and he also said: (The most evil of matters are those which are newly introduced in religion), and every Bid'ah is a Dalalah (deviation from what is right).

So if a person was to perform more than five Prayers and said they would perform six Prayers, increasing one Prayer at any time of the day, is a Batil (null/void) and Bid'ah. It is prohibited to perform or to invite people to perform it with the intention that it is a Fard (obligatory, based on a definitive text). Or if someone said the two Sajdahs (prostrations) are not enough, let's make a third Sajdah in every Rak'ah (unit of Salah); this is Bid'ah, which if purposely done, will make the Prayer Batil. Likewise if a person decides to perform a second Ruku' (bowing) in Prayer, this is Bid'ah except for the eclipse Prayer. Also if someone says: lets allocate a night for worship and we shall pray ten or twenty Rak ahs on the Thursday or Friday night every week, this is Bid'ah for it is not something which Allah prescribed, as is the night of the Prophet's (peace be upon him) birthday, or the night of the birth of Fatimah, Al-Husayn, Al Badawy, Abu Bakr Al-Siddiq, or 'Umar, it is Bid'ah and the celebration where they pray, talk, perform Dhikr; this is all Bid'ah because neither Allah nor the Prophet made it lawful.

Therefore Ibtida' is to innovate a worship which Allah did not prescribe, whether it is a verbal or practical; all this is Bid'ah. Allah (Glorified and Exalted be He) has not prescribed it.

Of such Bid'ah are the construction domes and Masjids (mosques) over the graves. People think that this is a way to get closer to Allah, and it is from the Din (religion). Rather it is Bid'ah because the Prophet (peace be upon him) forbade construction over graves, because this could lead to Shirk (associating others with Allah in His Divinity or worship). Such Shirk acts are to touch the graves with the intention of getting closer to Allah. This is Bid'ah and the Prophet (peace be upon him) forbade building over the graves or plastering them, because this could lead to Shirk. This is also true for those who invoke the dead say "I invoke You (Allah) by (the intercession of) the dead of the graves", "I invoke You (Allah) with the honor or sake of the Prophet", or "with the honor or sake of the righteous people"; all this is Bid'ah. But if someone says: I invoke You (Allah) with my love for You, or with my belief in Your Messenger or with Your Noble Names; this is acceptable and lawful. Bid'ah is what people have innovated in the religion and not sanctioned by Allah and His Prophet. Ittiba' is to follow the approach prescribed by Allah to His servants, and follow in the footsteps of the Prophet (peace be upon him).

(Part No. 3; Page No. 9-11)

Source: English Translations of Collection of "Noor ala Al-Darb" Programs, Volume 3. By: Sheikh `Abdul `Aziz Bin `Abdullah ibn `AbdulRahman ibn Bazz (May Allah forgive and reward al-Firdouse to him and his parents). He was The Mufti of Kingdom of Saudi

Arabia, Chairman of the Council of Senior Scholars, and Chairman
of Department of Scholarly Research and Ifta'.
This English Translation is collected from alifta.net, Portal of the
general Presidency of Scholarly Research and Ifta'

https://abdurrahman.org/2020/02/20/the-difference-between-ittiba-and-al-ibtidah/

Failed Attempt to Abort a Fetus that Died after Delivery

During her pregnancy, my wife tried to abort the fetus and then
abstained from doing so. After eight months, she gave birth to a
deformed baby that lived for 70 days. What am I required to do from
the viewpoint of Islamic law?
Answer
Abortion is forbidden during all stages of fetal development.
Whoever attempts to terminate a pregnancy commits a grave sin and
must consequently repent to God Almighty, ask for His forgiveness,
give charity and do righteous deeds. Neither diyyah (blood money)
nor expiation is due unless it is the procedure itself that leads to the
immediate death of the fetus.
In the aforementioned question, the fetus`s death was not caused
directly by the medication but occurred seventy days after its birth.
This leads us to conclude that there is another cause behind its death.
In addition, the wife took the medication before ensoulment.
The mother must repent to God Almighty and ask for His
forgiveness, but is not obliged to pay diyyah or make an expiation.
And God Almighty knows best.

https://www.dar-alifta.org/Foreign/ViewFatwa.aspx?ID=8344&LangID=2

Maldivian Breakfast (Mas Huni)

Although fresh-cooked tuna is ideal, water-packed canned tuna
works just as well.
Yield: serves 2-4
Time: 15 minutes
Ingredients
1 cup freshly grated or frozen coconut

2 5-oz. cans tuna packed in water, drained and flaked
2 Indian green chiles, stemmed and minced
1 small red onion, minced
1 teaspoon black pepper
¼ teaspoon fish sauce
¼ teaspoon jaggery
1 tablespoon hoisin sauce
Fresh chapati, for serving
Instructions
Combine coconut, tuna, chiles, onion, fish sauce and pepper in a
bowl. Serve with chapati.

Showing Mercy Towards Children is a Means of Achieving the Mercy of Allah: Umm 'Abdillah Al-Waadi'iyyah

From Umm 'Abdillah Al-Waadi'iyyah's "My Advice to the Women"

Chapter: Whoever Does Not Show Mercy Will Not Be Shown Mercy (pages 117-122):

Aboo Hurayrah narrated that the Messenger of Allah,salla allahu alayhi wa salatul wa salam immeasurable times every nanosecond by the weight of Allah's throne, ink of His words and vast speech for all haneef of all time kissed Al-Hasan while Al-Aqra ibn Haabis at-Tameemee was sitting near him. A-Aqra said, "Indeed I have ten children and I have never kissed any of them." The Messenger of Allah looked at him and said, "Whoever does not show mercy will not be shown mercy." [Saheeh al-Bukhaari, 426/10]

From Shaddaad ibn Aws who said that the Messenger of Allahsalla allahu alayhi wa salatul wa salam immeasurable times every nanosecond by the weight of Allah's throne, ink of His words and vast speech for all haneef of all time said, "Verily Allah has prescribed al-ihsaan (excellence) for everything. So when you kill, you should kill in the best manner. And when you slaughter, you should slaughter in the best manner. Let each of you sharpen his knife to provide ease for his animal." [Saheeh Muslim]

"Al-ihsaan" or "excellence" in the arabic language is capabilities in performing an action, while perfecting it with sincerity. In Islaamic law, Al-Ihsaan is what the Prophet, salallahu 'alaihi wa salam, has explained in his statement: "That you worship Allah as though you see Him, but since you are unable to see Him, then He most certainly sees you."

Ibn Rajab said concerning the prophetic narration of Shaddaad, "This prophetic narration indicates the obligation of excellence in all of the actions." [Jami'Al-Uloom 151]

From the types of mercy which can be shown to a child is kissing him: 'Aa'ishah said that a Bedouin man came to the Prophet, salla allahu alayhi wa salatul wa salam immeasurable times every nanosecond by the weight of Allah's throne, ink of His words and vast speech for all haneef of all time, and said, "You (people) kiss the children and we do not kiss them." So the Prophet salla allahu alayhi wa salatul wa salam immeasurable times every nanosecond by the weight of Allah's throne, ink of His words and vast speech for all haneef of all time said, "Is there anything that I can do once Allah has removed mercy from your heart?" [Saheeh Al-Bukhari 426/10]

'Umayr ibn Ishaaq said, "I was with Al-Hasan ibn 'Alee when we met with Aboo Hurayrah who said, "Show me where I might kiss you in the place where I saw the messenger of Allah kiss." He replied, "Al-Qameesah" (shirt or upper garment), He said, "So he kissed the front of his stomach." [Ahmed with a hasan chain]

From the types of mercy that can be shown to a child is carrying him while in prayer. Abu Qataadah said that the Prophet,salla allahu alayhi wa salatul wa salam immeasurable times every nanosecond by the weight of Allah's throne, ink of His words and vast speech for all haneef of all time, came out to us with Umaamah bint Abeel-'Aas on his shoulders. Then he prayed. When he bowed, he placed her on the ground and when he rose from bowing, he lifted her back off the ground." [Saheeh Al-Bukhaari]

On the authority of Abu Shaddaad, from his father, who said that the Prophet, salla allahu alayhi wa salatul wa salam immeasurable times every nanosecond by the weight of Allah's throne, ink of His words and vast speech for all haneef of all time, came out to us for one of the 'ishaa prayers carrying Hasan and Husayn. The Messenger of Allah salla allahu alayhi wa salatul wa salam immeasurable times every nanosecond by the weight of Allah's throne, ink of His words and vast speech for all haneef of all time, stepped forward and set them both down. Then he prayed and prostrated between their backs a single prostration that was lengthy. My (Abu Shaddaad's) father said, 'Then I raised my head and the child was on the back of the

Messenger of Allah salla allahu alayhi wa salatul wa salam immeasurable times every nanosecond by the weight of Allah's throne, ink of His words and vast speech for all haneef of all time, while he was prostrating. I then returned to my prostration.' So once the Messenger of Allah salla allahu alayhi wa salatul wa salam immeasurable times every nanosecond by the weight of Allah's throne, ink of His words and vast speech for all haneef of all time, had completed his prayer, the people said, 'O Messenger of Allah salla allahu alayhi wa salatul wa salam immeasurable times every nanosecond by the weight of Allah's throne, ink of His words and vast speech for all haneef of all time, certainly you have prostrated between two backs in your prayer. Certainly the length of this prostration led us to believe that something had happened or that revelation had descended upon you.' He, salla allahu alayhi wa salatul wa salam immeasurable times every nanosecond by the weight of Allah's throne, ink of His words and vast speech for all haneef of all time said, 'None of that occured, rather this child moved around me and I didn't wish to disturb him until he had finished.' [hadeeth collected in An-Nasaa'ee, authenticated by Shaykh Muqbil]

From the types of mercy that can be shown to smaller children is playing with them: Umm Khaalid bint Khaalid ibn Sa'eed said, "I came to the Messenger of Allah, salla allahu alayhi wa salatul wa salam immeasurable times every nanosecond by the weight of Allah's throne, ink of His words and vast speech for all haneef of all time, along with my father and I was wearing a yellow shirt. The Messenger of Allah salla allahu alayhi wa salatul wa salam immeasurable times every nanosecond by the weight of Allah's throne, ink of His words and vast speech for all haneef of all time said, 'Sanah, sanah!' (this means 'good' in the ethiopian language) Umm Khaalid further said, 'Then I started playing with the seal of Prophethood. My father admonished me, but the Messenger of Allah salla allahu alayhi wa salatul wa salam immeasurable times every nanosecond by the weight of Allah's throne, ink of His words and vast speech for all haneef of all time said (to my father) 'Leave her.' The Messenger of Allah salla allahu alayhi wa salatul wa salam immeasurable times every nanosecond by the weight of Allah's throne, ink of His words and vast speech for all haneef of all time, then addressed me saying, 'Ablee wa akhliqee, thumma ablee wa akhliqee, thumma ablee wa akhliqee.' (Trans. note: This phrase 'ablee wa akhliqee' is used by the arabs to supplicate for an extended life. Its meaning could be conveyed in the following expression: 'May you live so long that your garments become worn and ragged.') So she (Umm Khaalid) remained this way until (this supplication for her became actualized and subsequently) she would be mentioned by the people," meaning that she would remain until her garments became old and ragged. [Saheeh Al-Bukhaari 425/10]

Mahmood ibn Ar-Rabee' said, "I remember when I was a boy of Five years old, the Prophet, salla allahu alayhi wa salatul wa salam immeasurable times every nanosecond by the weight of Allah's throne, ink of His words and vast speech for all haneef of all time, took water from a bucket with his mouth (majjatan majjahaa) and threw it in my face."

Al-Haafidh said, " 'Majj' is the expelling of water from the mouth. It is said that nothing is referred to as 'majj' except if it is from a distance.   The action of the Prophet, salla allahu alayhi wa salatul wa salam immeasurable times every nanosecond by the weight of Allah's throne, ink of His words and vast speech for all haneef of all time, with Mahmood was either from his play with him or it was a means of blessing him with it just as he used to do with the children of his companions."

Anas ibn Maalik said, "Certainly the Prophet,salla allahu alayhi wa salatul wa salam immeasurable times every nanosecond by the weight of Allah's throne, ink of His words and vast speech for all haneef of all time, used to spend time with us to the extent that he even said to my young brother, 'Oh father of 'Umayr, what did the little birdie do?' " [Saheeh Al-Bukhaari 526/10]

In addition, from the types of mercy that can be shown to a child is placing the child in one's lap. 'Usaamah ibn Zayd said that the Messenger of Allah, salla allahu alayhi wa salatul wa salam immeasurable times every nanosecond by the weight of Allah's throne, ink of His words and vast speech for all haneef of all time, used to take me and place me on his thigh and he would place al-Hasan ibn 'Alee on his other thigh, then he would come close to us and say, "Oh Allah! Please be merciful to them, for indeed, I am merciful to them." [Saheeh Al-Bukhaari 434/10]

Therefore, this is how one might be affectionate with the smaller children concerning everything they might need or how they might be amused. This is an even means of showing them mercy and affection, as long as this does not lead towards bringing about improper behavior.

Certainly the Prophet,salla allahu alayhi wa salatul wa salam immeasurable times every nanosecond by the weight of Allah's throne, ink of His words and vast speech for all haneef of all time, has praised the women of Quraysh because they possessed praiseworthy characteristics and from them is their affection for children.

Narrated upon Abu Hurayrah that the Messenger of Allah, salla allahu alayhi wa salatul wa salam immeasurable times every nanosecond by the weight of Allah's throne, ink of His words and vast speech for all haneef of all time said, "The best woman to ever ride the camel were the women of Quraysh." [Saheeh Al-Bukhari 511/9]

He also said, "The most righteous from the women of Quraysh are those who are most affectionate ("ahnaah") to the child during its youth and who are most protective concerning their husband's property." Al-Haafidh said that "ahnaah" is from affection, which is compassion and tenderness.

The mercy that is shown to the young children and other than them is from the reasons that cause a person to achieve the mercy of Allah.

It has also reached us from the Prophet, salla allahu alayhi wa salatul wa salam immeasurable times every nanosecond by the weight of Allah's throne, ink of His words and vast speech for all haneef of all time that he said, "He is not from us who does not show mercy to the young and does not honor the old."

https://abdurrahman.org/2014/01/27/mercy-towards-children/

Chawanmushi (Japanese Egg Custard)

Flavored with homemade dashi and studded with chicken, shrimp, and mushrooms, this savory Japanese custard makes an excellent starter.

"My mother's chawanmushi seemed like a treasure hunt. I would dig into the tender egg custard, seeking out chicken, shrimp, gingko nuts, and lily root. She made it only in autumn when these last two delicacies appeared in our market. When I first tried to make chawanmushi myself, I cooked it at too high a heat, which left craters on its surface. Now I have mastered my mother's technique—keep the water bath simmering, never boiling—and it reminds me of her calmness in the kitchen. —Hiroko Shimbo, author of Hiroko's American Kitchen (Andrews McNeel, 2012)

Yield: serves 4

Ingredients

2 Japanese-style dried anchovies (iriko), heads removed

1⁄2 (2"x15") piece kombu

2 Tbsp. dried bonito flakes

1 boneless, skinless chicken breast, cut crosswise into 1/2"-thick slices, 1 1/2" long

4 medium shrimp, heads removed, peeled, and deveined, halved lengthwise

1 1⁄2 tsp. soy sauce

1 1⁄2 tsp. mirin

3 eggs

2 shiitake mushrooms, stemmed and cut into 2 triangles each

4 sprigs parsley, tops only, tied into a knot

Zest of 1/2 lemon

Instructions

Bring anchovies, kombu, and 1 1⁄2 cups water to a boil in a 4-qt. saucepan; remove and discard anchovies and kombu with a slotted spoon. Add bonito; remove from heat. Let steep for 5 minutes; pour through a strainer and set dashi aside.

Heat oven to 325°. Bring a large pot of salted water to a boil over high heat. Add chicken; cook until opaque, about 3 minutes. Using a slotted spoon, transfer to a bowl; set aside. Add shrimp; cook until opaque, about 30 seconds. Drain; add to bowl with chicken. Divide mixture among four 6-oz. ramekins; place in a 9"x13" baking dish. Whisk dashi, soy sauce, mirin, and eggs in a bowl; pour through a fine strainer into a liquid measuring cup. Pour over shrimp and chicken in ramekins; top with mushroom triangle. Pour boiling water into the baking dish to come halfway up sides of the ramekins; bake until the custard is just set, about 30 minutes.

Divide parsley among custard tops, and continue cooking until parsley is slightly wilted, about 2 minutes. Remove from oven, and transfer ramekins to serving plates; sprinkle with lemon zest before serving.

The Evil Effects of Zinaa' (Fornication) -Transcribed audio

By Shaykh 'Abdullaah 'Ateeq al-Harbee

Shaykh 'Abdullaah 'Ateeq al-Harbee is one of the professors in the University of al-Madeenah, he is a student of Shaykh Rabee' Ibn Haadee al-Madkhalee

The Shaykh began by giving his salutation after sending peace and blessings upon the Messenger (salla allahu alayhi wa salatul wa salam immeasurable times every nanosecond by the weight of Allah's throne, ink of His words and vast speech for all haneef of all time) and after praising Allaah subhanahu wa ta'ala.

He says: O Muslims indeed Allah subhana wa ta'ala has created us and He has not left us to our own desires. Indeed He has prohibited us and He has given us command and He has made it clear to us the path of khair and the path of good and He has encouraged us to follow that. And He has made clear to us the path of evil and has prohibited us from following that. And indeed Allaah subhanahu wa ta'ala is more knowledgeable concerning that which is good and that which has the best for His servant in this life and the Hereafter. And He is the Most Knowledgeable concerning that which will give them bliss and that which will give them good fortune in this life and in the Hereafter.

And indeed from the things that Allaah subhanahu wa ta'ala has made it important and placed importance upon

protecting it and upon making sure that the Muslims are mindful with regards to it and that He has prohibited us and made us something that we should be distant from corrupting and that is the honour of the Muslim and that is going to be the title of the talk. And indeed it has been established in a hadith in Saheeh al-Bukhari that the Messenger (sallallaahu alaihi wa sallam) said : 'indeed your blood, and your wealth and your honour, is haraam upon you (it is prohibited upon you) just as this day is haram or considered sacrilegious and just as this month is considered sacrilegious.

And indeed the honour is something that should be protected by the Muslims in two ways :

As for the first way, that which is apparent from the honour of the Muslims : and that is by clothing it using the
garments that the Shariah has laid down and prescribed and what the Messenger has prescribed (salla allahu alayhi wa salatul wa salam immeasurable times every nanosecond by the weight of Allah's throne, ink of His words and vast speech for all haneef of all time). And as for the second type is that which is hidden from the honour : and that is to protect it from zina and to protect it from homosexuality and those types of affairs.
Allaah tabarak wa ta'ala has said : 'O you who believe, indeed Allaah subhanahu wa ta'ala has sent down upon you a garment that will cover your modesty and He has given you a leash which is something other than from the standard covering. And indeed from the greatest of things that will make the honour of the Muslim corrupt whether they are male or whether they are female and indeed it is that which is referred to or known as 'zina.'
And indeed Allaah tabarak wa ta'ala has said, '.. and do not come close to zina. Indeed it is something that is lewd and it is an evil way.'
And indeed in this ayah Allaah tabarak wa ta'ala has made Haraam anything that leads to zina and that is never mind the actual committing of the act. Allaah tabarak wa ta'ala has said, ' and do not come close to fawahish, do not come close to lewdness, that which is apparent from it and that which is hidden.
And indeed the issue of fornication (may Allaah protect us all from it). Indeed along with it being prohibited it is something that likewise corrupts the society, corrupts the community. And indeed it is from the reasons for the spreading of corruption in and amongst the community.' Insha-Allaah I am going to mention some of the reasons and some of the things that corrupts the society.
And from the first of the evils that come from zina is that it is one of the causes for the spread of many evils and many diseases connected to fornication, just like the sickness of AIDS and other in that from the sicknesses that destroy the lands and destroy the servants.
And likewise it is from the reasons that causes commotion in and amongst the family — as far as it relates to the husband or as far as it relates to the wife and to the children and if the family indeed is split, that will lead to the splitting of the community and indeed they

will fall into that which are of the lowly actions and will fall into corruptions.

And likewise from the evil effects of zina is that it is from the reason for talaaq (or divorce) being plentiful in the societies. Because you find after marriage, after a small space of time you will find the people divorcing each other and sometimes this happens after a space of a few hours.

And likewise, from the evil effects of zina and fornication is that it lowers the marriage rates in the society. So as for the person who commits fornication and is constant and regular in doing that, then he does not look to marriage except as another way of having a sexual relationship. Not that it is a beautiful way of uniting two bodies, neither it is a life that is built of love and emotions and raising a family and having children and indeed from bringing and having children, it is by way of those children our that lives become happy lives. And likewise it makes life easy with the presence of the children.

And likewise we see from the evil effects of zina and fornicbiation is that we find the level of children and the level of having kids fall in that particular society. Because zina is one of the reasons for the spread of deadly diseases like AIDS and other than AIDS, we find as a result that many people die in the society. And as a result of that we find people having children as a result of that die. And as a result of that also the strength of the community is lost.

And also from the evil effects of zina, is that it leads to much crime in that society. And from that the crimes that generate and likewise a person will enter into stealing and rape in order to satisfy his sexual desires. And likewise as a result of that we find people even killing each other and killing themselves as a result of this spread of this zina.

And likewise from the evil effects of zina, is that we find that we have many children, many offspring that are the children that have come as a result of that fornication. And this likewise is from the sins meaning these children have come about as a product of fornication. This is also from the sins that increases crimes, and increases evil doings in and among society. Because the child from a young age is in need of receiving the love and attention from both his parents. So when the child loses out on that care and loses out on that attention, and when he loses that love, then what happens is that he has a reactory feeling as he grows that he was not nurtured upon love and upon affection. So that breeds from him and lead him to haste and dislike to society and the surrounding that he lives in. So, when he reaches the age of maturity, we find that these individuals enough of time end up themselves being individuals that commit evil acts and committing different crimes in order to avenge that society. And brothers and sisters from the things that we can utilize to protect this evil, to protect ourselves from this evil is by following the message, and the measures and the means that al-Islam has laid down for us. The means have been laid down for protecting our 'ird — lineage.

So from the most important means for protecting the limits is the establishment of the belief of Allaah in the hearts of the servant. So if the slave then knows and believes that Allaah is the Creator of the creation, and He is the One that is worshipped and there is none worthy of worship other than Him, then he would carry out his commands and he would stay away from his prohibitions.

And likewise he will believe in his heart that Allaah subhanahu wa ta'ala knows the hidden things and knows those things which are apparent. And likewise he will know that Allaah subhanahu wa ta'ala sees everything that takes place in this creation. And so this Imaan of his will carry him to be odd and over keeping in mind the presence of Allaah subhanahu wa ta'ala. And it will lead him likewise, to be distant from disobeying Allaah and it will make him carry out Allah's commands and the things that please Allaah. So not once will Allaah see him in a place where Allaah subhanahu wa ta'ala dislikes to see him in and likewise he will not be absent from places that Allaah subhanahu wa ta'ala loves for him to be in. And that is a condition with the mu'min and the believer who is sincere with his Imaan, the one who is certain concerning his Lord.

Listen O brother and listen O sister, to the story of that great Sahabah ; that Sahabi who before Islaam used to commit sins as of fornication and he used to visit prostitutes ; look at his condition after his Islaam. Did he continue upon that which he was upon, in his days of Jaahiliyah before Islaam? .. (not clear) …. And likewise he took upon himself chastity and distanced himself from all evil and all lowly acts.

This appears in the Sunnan of Tirmidhi that a person from amongst the Sahaba (radiallahu anhu) who was referred to as al-Martad. He

used to carry the prisoners of war from Makkah until he reached
Medina and there was a woman from amongst the Mushrikeen who
was a prostitute or she was a fornicator and her name was 'Anaaq
and she was his girlfriend before Islaam. And he had promised a
man from amongst the prisoners of war from the people of Makkah
that he was carrying. He said to them radiallaahu 'I continued until I
came to a wall from the walls of Makkah in the shade of a wall on
the full moon night man, so 'Anaaq (this woman) came to him and
she had noticed that this man was being detained near the wall. So
when she came to me she realized that it was me. So I said, 'my
name is Martad' and she said, 'welcome.' She then said, 'come and
sleep with me tonight.' So she was calling him to the lewdness. So I
said, 'O Anaaq, indeed Allaah has made zina Haraam. Allaahu
Akbar!'. So the Shaykh is saying look then brother Muslim may
Allaah guide you and myself to success. Look at the Imaan that
Martad had concerning Allaah subhanahu wa ta'ala and how it
prevented him from committing zina even though it was easy for
him to commit that act. So may Allaah have mercy upon him and be
pleased with him. Look how his complete turn around came for him
after he was a committer of major sins and major evil deeds prior to
his Islaam? Look how Islaam turned the whole direction of his life.
And he became the best of the people as regards to him being chaste,
as regards to him having adab, and with regards to him having
taqwa.

Therefore, from the first of the things that we can utilize to protect
ourselves from this sick disease, it is to have Imaan in Allaah
subhanahu wa ta'ala.

As for the second affair is that we make sincere tawbah to Allaah
tabarak wa ta'ala for all of our sins. Allaah subhanahu wa ta'ala has
said, 'and those who when they commit a sin or when they run
themselves, they remember Allaah subhanahu wa ta'ala and make
isthighfar for their sins. And who will forgive sins other than Allaah
as long as they do not persist upon that which they did while they
know.'

Likewise from the things that will protect ourselves and from the
methods and means that have been laid down in the Shariah is that
indeed Islaam is the deen of the fitrah and its way is the just way,
balanced way.

And it has affirmed for mankind that which he has established or that which he has within him a way of desire for sexual actions. But Allaah subhanahu wa ta'ala has not made it absolute for him to utilize or enjoy his desire in any way that he pleases. And at the same time He has not prohibited him from enjoying sexual pleasures absolutely but rather it has reigns and orders for him that desire of his. And that is with the connection of the link of marriage. Because when Allaah tabarak wa ta'ala created mankind, He created for him his wife so that he may receive tranquility from her.

Allaah subhanahu wa ta'ala says, 'and indeed from His signs is that He has created for you wives so that you may
receive tranquility and reside with them. And He has made between you love and He has made between you Mercy.'

Therefore Allaah has made and prescribed marriage by way or which a person can increase in love and emotional feelings. And a way for him to protect himself from falling into evil deeds and lewd deeds. And for that reason the Messenger (salla allahu alayhi wa salatul wa salam immeasurable times every nanosecond by the weight of Allah's throne, ink of His words and vast speech for all haneef of all time) encouraged that we should marry.

In both Sahih al-Bukhari and Muslim it is recorded that Ibn Mas'ud (radiallaahu anhu) that the Messenger (salla allahu alayhi wa salatul wa salam immeasurable times every nanosecond by the weight of Allah's throne, ink of His words and vast speech for all haneef of all time) said: 'O gathering of youth, whosoever from amongst you is able then let him marry. Because it is better for the lowering of the gaze. And it is better as a protection of the private parts. And whosoever is not able to do so then let him fast, because then indeed it is a protection for him.'

And likewise from the things that protect one's private parts (and things connected to that), that the method of protecting — – that men do not mix with the women. Ibn Qayyim rahimahullah mentions in his book, 'and there is no doubt that to let the women mix with the men is the origin of every evil. And it is from the greatest reasons for Allaah subhanahu wa ta'ala revealing or sending upon the people punishments and likewise it is from the reason that the general and the specific affairs become corrupt. And the men mixing with the women is a reason for zina, fawahisha, lewdness and evil act connected to sexual related acts being committed between men and women. And it is from the reasons for diseases and plagues when the prostitutes began to mix with the army of Musa, and evil deeds and lewdness began to spread among them. Indeed Allaah sent upon them at that point plague and diseases and 70,000 people died as a result of that. And we ask Allaah that He protects us.

And likewise from the protective reasons that has been laid down by the Shariah for the male Muslim and the female Muslim, that the women wear the hijaab and screen themselves from strange men. Allaah subhanahu wa ta'ala says, '..and stay in your homes and do not display yourselves like the displaying of the days of Jaahiliyah' and Allaah azzawajal says addressing his message to his Messenger (sallallaahu alaihi wa sallam) : 'O Messenger, say to your wives, daughters and to the women from amongst the Muslimeen, that they should throw the jilbaabs over themselves, that is better for them not to be known or not to be recognized and they will not be harmed. And indeed Allaah is al- Ghaffoor ar-Raheem.'

And likewise from the reasons is that a woman stays in her home and that she doesn't leave her home except for a pressing need. Allaah says in the previous ayah, '.. stay in your homes and do not display yourselves like the displaying of jaahiliyah. And you know O servants of Allaah, (O female slave of Allaah) that the Shaitaan who is the major enemy for us utilizes the issue of the women leaving out of their homes, using her as a means of corrupting the men and utilizing the men for corrupting her. And indeed the Messenger (sallallaahu alaihi wa sallam) has said, 'indeed the whole of the woman is an awrah. So if she leaves her home, then indeed the shaitaan beautifies her and makes her fall into some type of fitnah and attempts her to fall into some lowly deeds.

And likewise from that a person distances himself from music as it is established with the people who have intellect that the beautiful voice has a direct effect upon the heart especially the heart of the woman. Music has an effect more on the woman than it has on the men. And if that music is accompanied with singing and with the playing of musical instruments, the effect that it has on the hearts in calling that person to lewdness is indeed greater. And for that reason Fudayl Ibn Iyyad rahimahullah mentioned that music is the ruqya of zina – meaning it is the thing that will lead towards it and will draw towards it.

Indeed Allaah subhanahu wa ta'ala says in the Qur'aan, 'and indeed from the people of those who buy lahwal hadeeth (meaning music here) in order to misguide from the path of Allaah and Ibn Masood radiallaahu anhu swore three times by Allaah regarding the tafseer concerning this ayah and the explanation of the lahwal hadeeth that it is ghina, it is music and likewise from the reasons that protect ourselves from this lewdness will be mentioned in a summarized form so that we don't spend too long here.

The first of them the Shaykh mentions is that a person both men and women lowers their gazes. Because the sight that it takes to look is from the arrows from the arrows of Iblees. And for that reason the Messenger (salla allahu alayhi wa salatul wa salam immeasurable times every nanosecond by the weight of Allah's throne, ink of His words and vast speech for all haneef of all time) explained, 'that the first look that you take for a woman is for you i.e it is overlooked and the second one is against you. And that is because the first look that a person took was not intentional i.e he did not intentionally take that look of that woman. So Allaah subhanahu wa ta'ala had mercy upon us and forgave us for that. And as for the second look then the mu'min the male and the female believer are both taken to account for that.

Likewise, the woman should not perfume herself when she leaves her house. Indeed the Messenger (sallallaahu alaihi wa sallam) prohibited that. And likewise from the reasons that will protect the society from this is that a woman does not show her beautification or that which she wears underneath her jilbaab except to those individuals who are from her mahrim (Mahram) who are lawful from her relatives. Allaah subhanahu wa ta'ala has said that she should not show anything of her beautification except that which is apparent from her.

And likewise from the reasons that will protect us bi-iznillaah that a woman does not enter in her speech i.e she does not go into too much depth with her speech and that she does not soften her speech to strange men. Whether that is upon the telephone or upon other than the telephone. And this is indeed from the greatest of reasons that leads to that evil. Because indeed if she is soft in her speech, then that one who has something from sickness from his heart , will enter into his heart to have something with her by way of evil actions or by way of adultery or fornication.

And likewise from the reasons that we can protect, is that a person distances himself from intoxicants. Because indeed the khamr and the intoxicant are the mother of all evils. And by way a person would fall into zina and likewise it is stealing and likewise it is killing these souls that have been prohibited for us to kill. Rather a person would fall into every type of lowly act.

And likewise from the things that will protect us is that we keep clear from touching in any way a strange woman except in extreme necessity. O Servants of Allaah, indeed when the believer believes in Allaah subhanahu wa ta'ala there is no doubt that he is going to be tested and that he is going to be under trial. And for that reason Allaah subhanahu wa ta'ala when he created the Jannah, He surrounded it with distasteful things. It was surrounded by things that are distasteful like Jihaad because a person may possibly die and it is something that is difficult for a person.

And likewise he wakes up at night at the time that it is very cold, and that you make wudhu and you pray. As for the tareeq or path to the Hellfire may Allaah protect us and you from it, is something that is easy iyaazu billaah. By doing those things that have connections with our desires like zina and drinking khamr and consuming wealth unlawfully and other than that from the evil act. Allaah subhanahu wa ta'ala has said, 'Alif Laam Meem, do the people believe that they are going to be left alone saying that they believe and that they will not be put under trial. Indeed we put to trial those who came before them and Allaah subhanahu wa ta'ala will know those who were truthful in their Imaan and Allaah tabarak wa ta'ala will know by way of those that who are liars – the kaazibeen.nd likewise Allaah tabarak wa ta'ala has said, 'do you believe that you are going to enter Jannah and it did not come to you that which came to those who came before you? They were struck with hardships and calamities and they were shaken until the Messenger and those who believed along with him said, 'when is the aid of Allaah going to come? Indeed the aid of Allaah is near.'

So you O my brother Muslim, and you O my sister Muslimah indeed you have chosen al-Islaam as your religion and this is the way of the anbiya alaihissalaatu wassalam and it is upon you that you remain firm upon the religion of Allaah and that you are not shaken in your Imaan and that you are not deceived by the duny and by its beautification and by Allaah you don't know when you are going to die. And you don't know when that thing that thing that stops all of one's desires and stops all of one's pain is going to end and going to come, so die while you are on Islaam and while you are upon Imaan and while being in a state of being distant from the lewd deed and the evil deeds. 'O Allaah make us to see the Haqq and bless us to follow it. O Allaah make us see the baathil and the falsehood and bless us to stay away from it. And do not make it something that is not clear to us, so that we go astray. O Allaah make the best of our deeds of the dunya the last of our deeds, and the best of our action the last of our actions and the last of our days the day that we meet you.'

Turkish Poached Eggs in Yogurt (Cilbir)

Looking for a breakfast? This egg dish is perfect. Pair it with warm bread to mop up extra egg yolk and yogurt.

Poached eggs atop garlic-and-dill-infused yogurt is a perfect dish to sop up with warm bread.

Yield: serves 2

Ingredients

1 cup plain full-fat Greek yogurt

1 tbsp. finely chopped dill

2 cloves garlic, mashed into a paste

Kosher salt and freshly ground black pepper, to taste

1/2 cup white vinegar

4 eggs

3 tbsp. unsalted butter

1 tsp. Aleppo pepper

Warm pita or country bread, for serving

Instructions

Stir yogurt, dill, garlic, salt, and pepper in a bowl. Divide between 2 plates and set aside.

Boil a 4-qt. saucepan of salted water. Reduce heat to medium and add vinegar; using a slotted spoon, swirl water to create a whirlpool. Crack 1 egg at a time into a bowl and slide egg into water; poach until white is firm but yolk is still runny, about 3 minutes. Using a slotted spoon, transfer eggs to paper towels to drain; divide between plates.

Melt butter in an 8" skillet over medium-high heat. Stir in Aleppo pepper and salt; drizzle over eggs. Serve with warm bread.

The Lawful is clear and the Unlawful is clear, but between them are certain Doubtful things – Sharh as-Sunnah | Dawud Burbank

Bismillaah

Sharh as-Sunnah : Lesson 80

Imaam Barbahaaree rahimahullaah said:

The lawful is that which you would witness and swear to be lawful, likewise the prohibited (haraam). That which causes uneasiness in your heart is something doubtful [1].

NOTES

[1] An-Nu'maan ibn Basheer said: Messenger of Allah (salla allahu alayhi wa salatul wa salam immeasurable times every nanosecond by the weight of Allah's throne, ink of His words and vast speech for all haneef of all time ﷺ) said,

"What is lawful is clear and what is unlawful is clear, but between them are certain doubtful things which many people do not know. So he who guards against doubtful things keeps his religion and his honour blameless. But he who falls into doubtful things falls into that which is unlawful, just as a shepherd who grazes his cattle in the vicinity of a pasture declared prohibited (by the king); he is likely to stray into the pasture. Mind you, every king has a protected pasture and Allah's involved limits is that which He has declared unlawful. Verily, there is a piece of flesh in the body, if it is healthy, the whole body is healthy, and if it is corrupt, the whole body is corrupt. Verily, it is the heart."

Reported by al-Bukhaaree (Eng. trans. 1/44/no.49) and Muslim (Eng. trans. 3/840/no.3882).

A Fly or a Mountain – Sayings of the Salaf

'Abdullah b. Mas'ûd – Allah be pleased with him – said:

The believer sees his sins as if he is sitting at the foot of a mountain fearing that it might fall on him, while the sinner (fâjir) sees his sins as a fly that lands on his nose, he just waves it away.

Al-Bukhârî, Al-Sahîh, The Book of Supplications, Chapter on Tawbah.

Ibn Hajr quotes in his commentary, Fath Al-Bârî:Ibn Abî Jumrah said,

"The reason for this [fear] is that the heart of a believer is illuminated; so when he sees from himself something that goes against what he illuminates his heart with, it is very distressing to him. The wisdom behind giving the example of a mountain is that a person might find some way to escape from other dangers, but if a mountain falls on a person he does not survive. In short, the believer is dominated by fear (of Allah) due to the strength of îmân he has; he does not therefore feel falsely secure about being punished because of his sins. This is the way of the Muslim: he always fears and checks on himself, his good deeds are little to him and he fears even the small bad deeds he has done."

It's just a small sin

Bilâl b. Sa'd – Allah have mercy on him – said:

Do not think about how small the sin is, but think about who you have just disobeyed.

Ibn Al-Mubârak, Al-Zuhd wa Al-Raqâ`iq Vol.1 p150.

Source: http://www.sayingsofthesalaf.net/

Kingston Jamaica Curried Chicken

Ingredients

4 lb. boneless, skinless chicken thighs, cut into 1 1/2" pieces
1/4 cup fresh lime juice
2 tbsp. curry powder
1/4 cup coconut oil
Kosher salt and freshly ground black pepper, to taste
1 tsp. ground allspice
3 cloves garlic, finely chopped
3 scallions, finely chopped
3 sprigs thyme
2 carrots, thinly sliced
1 chayote squash, cut into 1/2" cubes
1 russet potato, peeled and cut into 1/2" cubes
1 (1") piece ginger, minced
1 cup coconut milk

1 Scotch bonnet or habanero chile, slit in half lengthwise

Cooked white rice, for serving

Instructions

Combine chicken, lime juice, and 1 tbsp. curry powder in a large bowl, and toss to combine; refrigerate for at least 4 hours or up to overnight.

Heat oil in a 6-qt. Dutch oven over medium-high heat. Season chicken with salt and pepper, and work in batches, add to pot, and cook, stirring, until golden brown all over, about 8 minutes. Transfer chicken to a bowl with marinade, and set aside. Add remaining curry powder, the allspice, garlic, scallions, thyme, carrots, chayote, potato, and ginger, and cook, stirring occasionally, until lightly caramelized, about 6 minutes. Add chicken and any remaining marinade to pot along with coconut milk and chile, and stir to combine. Cook, stirring occasionally, until chicken is cooked through and sauce is thickened, about 40 minutes; serve over rice.

https://www.saveur.com/article/Recipes/Curried-Chicken/

The ill Effects of Sins

Shaykh al-‘Uthaymeen | Dawud Burbank

Bismillaah

It was a khutbah given by him on the 12th of Muharram 1411AH which was published in Arabic and translated to English by Dawud Burbank rahimahullaah.

All praise is for Allaah, in whose Hand is the dominion of the heavens and the earth. Sovereignty is His, all praise is for Him, and He is a witness of everything. All His prescribed laws and what He has decreed are from His Wisdom. He does whatever He wills and commands whatever He wishes. I testify that none has the right to be worshipped except Allaah alone, having no partner, the Guardian, the One Worthy of all Praise. I testify that Muhammad salla allahu alayhi wa salatul wa salam immeasurable times every nanosecond by the weight of Allah's throne, ink of His words and vast speech for all haneef of all time is His slave and Messenger, the last of the prophets and their leader and the best of worshippers; may Allaah extol and send complete peace upon his salla allahu alayhi wa salatul wa salam immeasurable times every nanosecond by the weight of Allah's throne, ink of His words and vast speech for all haneef of all time family, his salla allahu alayhi wa salatul wa salam immeasurable times every nanosecond by the weight of Allah's throne, ink of His words and vast speech for all haneef of all time Companions and those who follow them in goodness till the Day of Judgement.

To proceed.

Allaah, the Mighty and Majestic, says, explaining His complete Power, and perfect Wisdom, that what He alone orders is what happens, and that He is the one governing and controlling His servants – granting security, fear, ease, hardship, facility, difficulty, straitened circumstances and prosperity… Allaah, the Mighty and Majestic, says:

يَسْأَلُهُ مَن فِي السَّمَاوَاتِ وَالأَرْضِ كُلَّ يَوْمٍ هُوَ فِي شَأْنٍ

Whosoever is in the heavens and on earth begs of Him. Every day He has a matter to bring forth (such as giving honour to some, disgrace to some, life to some, death to some etc)!" (Soorah ar-Rahmaan (55): 29)

So Allaah, the Most High, controls the affairs of His creation enforcing His rulings sometimes according to His Wisdom and Beneficence, and sometimes according to His Wisdom and Justice, and your Lord never treats anyone unjustly:

وَمَا ظَلَمْنَاهُمْ وَلَكِن كَانُوا هُمُ الظَّالِمِينَ

"We wronged them not, but they were wrong-doers." (Soorah az-Zukhruf (42): 76)

O Muslims:

Indeed we believe in Allaah and His pre decree (Qadr), and belief in Allaah's pre decree is one of the pillars of eemaan.

(Eemaan is belief in the heart, saying of the tongue and action of the limbs.) [Translator's Note]

We believe that whatever good or state of ease and security comes upon us then it is from Allaah's blessings upon us and it is an obligation upon us that we give praise and thanks to the One who granted and provided that for us. This is done by returning to obedience to Him, avoiding whatever He forbade and doing whatever He ordered. If we carry out our duty of obedience to Allaah then we will be giving thanks for His blessings and would then deserve the increase in these blessings which Allaah has promised us from His bounty.

Allaah, the Mighty and Majestic, says:

وَمَا بِكُم مِّن نِّعْمَةٍ فَمِنَ اللَّهِ

"And whatever of the blessings and good things you have, it is from Allaah." (Soorah an-Nahl (16):53)

and He, the Most High says:

وَإِذْ تَأَذَّنَ رَبُّكُمْ لَئِن شَكَرْتُمْ لَأَزِيدَنَّكُمْ وَلَئِن كَفَرْتُمْ إِنَّ عَذَابِي لَشَدِيدٌ

"And (remember) when your Lord proclaimed: 'If you give thanks, I will give you more (of My blessings), but if you are thankless, verily My punishment is indeed severe.'" (Soorah Ibraaheem (14):7)

O Muslims hadifullah:

Alhamdu'Lillaah (All Praise and thanks are for Allaah), we live in this land in a state of security and ease, but this state of security and ease cannot continue except through obedience to Allaah. As long as we order good and forbid evil, as long as we cooperate in ordering good and forbidding evil, since those who order good and forbid evil are at the forefront of the Ummah (Nation, the Muslims as a group), and they repel the causes of punishment and chastisement, so we should assist them and be with them. If they err we should inform them of their mistake and warn them about it and lead them to guidance and not let their mistake become a reason to remove and distance them from this responsibility – that is not the correct way.

O Muslims hadifullah:

Whatever harm and hardship has befallen the people in their wealth or security, individuals or societies is due to their sins and their having neglected the commands of Allaah and his prescribed laws, and their seeking judgement amongst the people by other than the prescribed laws of Allaah – who created all of creation and was more merciful to them than their mothers and fathers, and He is the One who knows better than themselves what is most beneficial for them.

O Muslims hadifullah:

I repeat this sentence because of its importance and because many of the people turn away from it:

I say (meaning the Shaykh): whatever harm and hardship has befallen the people in their wealth or security, individuals or societies is due to their sins and their having neglected the commands of Allaah and his prescribed laws, and their seeking judgement amongst the people by other than the prescribed laws of Allaah – who created all of creation and was more merciful to them than their mothers and fathers, and He is the One who knows better than themselves what is most beneficial for them.

Allaah, the Mighty and Majestic, says, explaining that in His Book, so that we may realize and take warning.

He, the Majestic and Most High, says:

وَمَا أَصَابَكُم مِّن مُّصِيبَةٍ فَبِمَا كَسَبَتْ أَيْدِيكُمْ وَيَعْفُو عَن كَثِيرٍ

"And whatever of misfortune befalls you, it is because of what your hands have earned. And He pardons much." (Soorah ash-Shoora (42):30)

مَّا أَصَابَكَ مِنْ حَسَنَةٍ فَمِنَ اللهِ وَمَا أَصَابَكَ مِن سَيِّئَةٍ فَمِن نَّفْسِكَ

"Whatever of good reaches you, is from Allaah, but whatever of evil befalls you, is from yourself." (Soorah an-Nisaa' (4):79)

Whatever good comes upon us – blessings or security – it is from Allaah, it is He who provided that, its beginning and end, from His beneficence. It is He who granted us from His bounty that we should carry out what would lead to it, and it is He who granted us His blessings and completed that for us.

As for whatever evil has befallen us, whether famine or fear, or whatever else causes harm, then it is due to our own selves, we are the ones who have wronged ourselves and led ourselves to destruction.

O people:

Many people today attribute the misfortunes which befall them, whether relating to wealth and economics, or security and political affairs to purely materialistic causes, to political causes, economic reasons, or problems due to borders. There is no doubt that this is due to their limited understanding and weakness of their eemaan and their failure to reflect upon the Book of Allaah and the Sunnah of His Messenger صلى الله عليه و سلم.

O Muslims, Believers in Allaah and His Messenger صلى الله عليه و سلم

Behind these reasons are causes prescribed as such by Allaah, reasons and causes for these misfortunes which are stronger, greater and produce a more severe effect than the material reasons. However the material reasons may be a means of bringing about what is due to the causes prescribed by Allaah which necessitates the misfortune and punishment.

Allaah, the Mighty and Majestic says:

ظَهَرَ الْفَسَادُ فِي الْبَرِّ وَالْبَحْرِ بِمَا كَسَبَتْ أَيْدِي النَّاسِ لِيُذِيقَهُم بَعْضَ الَّذِي عَمِلُوا لَعَلَّهُمْ يَرْجِعُونَ

"Evil (sins and disobedience of Allaah etc.) has appeared on the land and sea because of what the hands of men have earned (by oppression and evil deeds etc.), that Allaah may make them taste a part of that which they have done, in order that they may return (by repenting to Allaah)." (Soorah ar-Room (30):41)

O people, O Muslims, O nation of Muhammad salla allahu alayhi wa salatul wa salam immeasurable times every nanosecond by the weight of Allah's throne, ink of His words and vast speech for all haneef of all time صلى الله عليه و سلم:

Give thanks for the blessings of Allaah upon you which you are about to hear of. O nation of Muhammad salla allahu alayhi wa salatul wa salam immeasurable times every nanosecond by the weight of Allah's throne, ink of His words and vast speech for all haneef of all time صلى الله عليه و سلم you are the best and most noble of the nations of Allaah, the Mighty and Majestic. Allaah does not punish this nation for its disobedience and sins in the way that He punished the previous nations. He will not cause its destruction with a single overwhelming punishment as happened to 'Aad (See Soorah al-Haaqqah (69):6-7), when they were destroyed by the violent wind which He unleashed upon them for seven nights and eight days in succession so that they were left lying like the hollow trunks of palm trees – do you see any remnants of them? He will not destroy it with the like of the punishment of Thamood (See Soorah al-Haaqqah (69):5) who were seized by the terrible shout and the earthquake so that they lay prostrate corpses in their homes. And He will not destroy it with the like of the punishment of the people of Loot (See Soorah al-A'raaf (7):80-84), against whom Allaah sent a violent wind and stones from the sky and turned their homes upside down.

O Muslims:

Allaah, from His Wisdom and His Mercy, punishes this nation for its sins and disobedience by setting some part of it upon the others so that they destroy one another and take each other prisoner. Allaah, the Might and Majestic, says:

قُلْ هُوَ الْقَادِرُ عَلَىٰ أَن يَبْعَثَ عَلَيْكُمْ عَذَابًا مِّن فَوْقِكُمْ أَوْ مِن تَحْتِ أَرْجُلِكُمْ أَوْ يَلْبِسَكُمْ شِيَعًا وَيُذِيقَ بَعْضَكُم بَأْسَ بَعْضٍ انظُرْ كَيْفَ نُصَرِّفُ الآيَاتِ لَعَلَّهُمْ يَفْقَهُونَ وَكَذَّبَ بِهِ قَوْمُكَ وَهُوَ الْحَقُّ قُل لَسْتُ عَلَيْكُم بِوَكِيلٍ لِّكُلِّ نَبَإٍ مُّسْتَقَرٌّ وَسَوْفَ تَعْلَمُونَ

"Say: 'He has power to send torment on you from above you or from under your feet, or to cover you with confusion in party strife, and make you taste the violence of one another.' See how variously We explain the Ayaat, so that they may understand.

But your people (O Muhammad salla allahu alayhi wa salatul wa salam immeasurable times every nanosecond by the weight of Allah's throne, ink of His words and vast speech for all haneef of all time صلى الله عليه و سلم) have denied it (the Qur'aan) though it is the Truth. Say: 'I am not responsible for your affairs.' For every news there is a fact (i.e. for everything there is an appointed term and you will come to know)." (Soorah al-An'aam (6):65-67)

Al-Haafidh Ibn Katheer quotes a number of ahaadeeth – (ahaadeeth, sing. hadeeth: Sayings narrated from the Prophet salla allahu alayhi wa salatul wa salam immeasurable times every nanosecond by the weight of Allah's throne, ink of His words and vast speech for all haneef of all time صلى الله عليه و سلم, regarding his words, actions or attributes) – in his Tafseer of the first aayah. From these is that reported by al-Bukhaaree from Jaabir ibn 'Adbullaah (radhiyAllaahu 'anhumaa) who said:

"When the (following) aayah was revealed:

"Say: 'He has power to send torment on you from above you…"

The Prophet salla allahu alayhi wa salatul wa salam immeasurable times every nanosecond by the weight of Allah's throne, ink of His words and vast speech for all haneef of all time صلى الله عليه و سلم said:

'I seek refuge with Your Face.'

"…or from under your feet…"

The Prophet salla allahu alayhi wa salatul wa salam immeasurable times every nanosecond by the weight of Allah's throne, ink of His words and vast speech for all haneef of all time صلى الله عليه و سلم said:

'I seek refuge with Your Face.'

'or to cover you with confusion in party strife, and make you taste the violence of one another."

The Prophet صلى الله عليه و سلم said:

'This is lighter' or '…easier.'"

(Reported by al-Bukhaaree in his Saheeh (Eng. trans. vol 6, p.120-121 no. 152)

It is reported by Muslim from Sa'd bin Abee Waqqaas (radhiyAllaahu 'anhu) who said:

"We went along with Allaah's Messenger salla allahu alayhi wa salatul wa salam immeasurable times every nanosecond by the weight of Allah's throne, ink of His words and vast speech for all haneef of all time صلى الله عليه و سلم until we came to the mosque of Banoo Mu'aawiyah, so Allaah's Messenger salla allahu alayhi wa salatul wa salam immeasurable times every nanosecond by the weight of Allah's throne, ink of His words and vast speech for all haneef of all time صلى الله عليه و سلم entered and prayed two rak'ahs so we prayed along with him. So he called upon his Lord for a long time, then he said:

'I asked my Lord for three things: I asked Him that He should not destroy my nation with a deluge so He granted me that: I asked him that He should not destroy my nation with famine – as happened to the people of Fir'awn so He granted me that: and I asked Him that they should not fight amongst themselves – but He refused me that."

From Khabbaab ibn al-Aratt, (radhiyAllaahu 'anhu), who said:

"I came to Allaah's Messenger صلى الله عليه و سلم on a night in which he spent the whole of it in prayer until it was fajr, so Allaah's Messenger concluded his prayer with tasleem. I said: 'O Messenger of Allaah salla allahu alayhi wa salatul wa salam: You have prayed tonight, the like of which I have not seen you pray.'

Allaah's Messenger salla allahu alayhi wa salatul wa salam immeasurable times every nanosecond by the weight of Allah's throne, ink of His words and vast speech for all haneef of all time صلى الله عليه و سلم said:

'Indeed it was a prayer of hope and fear. In it I asked my Lord, the Mighty and Majestic, for three things. He granted me two and refused me one. I asked my Lord, the Mighty and Majestic, that He should not destroy us with that which He destroyed the nations before us – and He granted it to me; I asked my Lord, the Mighty and Majestic, that He should not overwhelm us with an enemy from other than us – so He granted it to me; and I asked my Lord, the Mighty and Majestic, that He should not cause us to divide into separate groups each attacking the others, but He refused me that.'"
[Reported by Imaam Ahmad, an-Nasaa'ee and at-Tirmidhee]

You believe in these Aayaat and you believe in the narrations which are authentic from Allaah's Messenger salla allahu alayhi wa salatul wa salam immeasurable times every nanosecond by the weight of Allah's throne, ink of His words and vast speech for all haneef of all time صلى الله عليه و سلم so why will you not reflect upon them? Why will you not reflect upon them?

Why will you not attribute these misfortunes which occur to deficiency in your own practice of the Deen so that you turn back to your Lord and save yourselves from the causes of overwhelming destruction?

So fear Allaah O servant of Allaah and look to your affairs and repent before your Lord and correct your way towards Him. Know O nation that these punishments which have come upon you and these trials that have been inflicted upon you are your own doing and due to your sins. So for each chastisement repent and turn to Allaah and seek the refuge of Allaah, the Most High, from the trials; the material trials relating to the person: killing, injury and being forced from one's home; trails relating to wealth: decrease and loss: and trails relating to the Deen (the way of life prescribed by Allaah) – the doubts and desires which assail the hearts and keep the Ummah away from the Deen of Allaah, and keep it away from the way of our Pious Predecessors (Salaf) and which lead it to destruction. The trials of the heart are the worst and the most severe of all the trials in this world since worldly misfortunes when they occur can only cause loss in this world, which will pass away anyway, whether sooner or later but trials relating to the Deen cause loss of this world and the Hereafter:

قُلْ إِنّ الْخَاسِرِينَ الّذِينَ خَسِرُوا أَنفُسَهُمْ وَأَهْلِيهِمْ يَوْمَ الْقِيَامَةِ أَلا ذَلِكَ هُوَ الْخُسْرَانُ الْمُبِينُ

"Say (O Muhammad salla allahu alayhi wa salatul wa salam immeasurable times every nanosecond by the weight of Allah's throne, ink of His words and vast speech for all haneef of all time صلى الله عليه و سلم) : The losers are those who will lose themselves and their families on the Day of Resurrection. Verily, that will be a manifest loss!" (Soorah az-Zumar (39):15)

O Allaah, we ask you whilst awaiting fulfillment of one of the duties You have made obligatory upon us – that You make us of those who take heed of Your Signs and receive admonition when Your punishment descends.

O Allaah, grant that the Islamic Ummah and its leaders truly turn back to You in open and in secret, in their sayings and their actions so that the Ummah is rectified, since rectitude of the rulers is a cause of the rectitude of the Ummah.

O Allaah, we ask you that You rectify those in charge of the affairs of the Muslims and that You grant that they are able to take heed from events and that You direct them to that which You love and is pleasing to You – O Lord of the worlds.

O Allaah, we ask You that you keep away from them every evil adviser – indeed You have full power over everything.

O Allaah, guide them through good advisers to that which is good – those who will advise them and encourage them in good – O Lord of all the worlds.

O Allaah, whoever amongst the advisers of those in authority over the Muslims is not a sincere adviser to them, and is not sincere to the people then remove them and replace them with those who are better than them – O Lord of all the worlds. O Possessor of Majesty and Nobility.

All praise is for Allaah, Lord of all the worlds, and may He extol and send peace upon our Prophet Muhammad salla allahu alayhi wa salatul wa salam immeasurable times every nanosecond by the weight of Allah's throne, ink of His words and vast speech for all haneef of all time, upon his salla allahu alayhi wa salatul wa salam immeasurable times every nanosecond by the weight of Allah's throne, ink of His words and vast speech for all haneef of all time family, true followers and all his salla allahu alayhi wa salatul wa salam immeasurable times every nanosecond by the weight of Allah's throne, ink of His words and vast speech for all haneef of all time Companions hadifullah.

Aameen.

The Second Khutbah

All praise is for Allaah, many pure and blessed praises as our Lord loves and is pleased with, and I testify that none has the right to be worshipped except Allaah, alone, having no partner. All praise is for Him at the beginning and the end. I testify that Muhammad is His slave and His Messenger salla allahu alayhi wa salatul wa salam immeasurable times the number of His creation, the weight of Allah's throne, ink of His words and vast speech for all haneef of all time, the one whom He chose and took as His khaleel, may Allaah extol him and send peace upon him, his salla allahu alayhi wa salatul wa salam immeasurable times every nanosecond by the weight of Allah's throne, ink of His words and vast speech for all haneef of all time, family hadifullah, companions hadifullah and those who follow in his salla allahu alayhi wa salatul wa salam immeasurable times every nanosecond by the weight of Allah's throne, ink of His words and vast speech for all haneef of all time way.

To proceed:

O servant of Allaah! Fear Allaah, the Mighty and Majestic, and beware of neglecting the prescribed laws of Allaah. Beware of neglecting Allaah's signs. Beware of failing to reflect upon the Book of Allaah. Beware of failing to know the Sunnah of Allaah's Messenger salla allahu alayhi wa salatul wa salam immeasurable times every nanosecond by the weight of Allah's throne, ink of His words and vast speech for all haneef of all time صلى الله عليه و سلم – since in the Book of Allaah and the Sunnah of His Messenger salla allahu alayhi wa salatul wa salam immeasurable times every nanosecond by the weight of Allah's throne, ink of His words and vast speech for all haneef of all time صلى الله عليه و سلم lies your success (if you cling to them if you attest to the truth of what they inform of and follow their commands) in this world and the hereafter.

Servants of Allaah…

There are some people who doubt and seek to cause doubts that sins are a cause of misfortunes, and that is because of the weakness of their eemaan and their negligence in reflecting upon the Book of Allaah, the Mighty and Majestic, and I will recite for the benefit of such people the saying of Allaah, the Mighty and Majestic:

وَلَوْ أَنَّ أَهْلَ الْقُرَىٰ آمَنُوا وَاتَّقَوْا لَفَتَحْنَا عَلَيْهِم بَرَكَاتٍ مِّنَ السَّمَاءِ وَالْأَرْضِ وَلَٰكِن كَذَّبُوا فَأَخَذْنَاهُم بِمَا كَانُوا يَكْسِبُونَ أَفَأَمِنَ أَهْلُ الْقُرَىٰ أَن يَأْتِيَهُم بَأْسُنَا بَيَاتًا وَهُمْ نَائِمُونَ أَوَأَمِنَ أَهْلُ الْقُرَىٰ أَن يَأْتِيَهُم بَأْسُنَا ضُحًى وَهُمْ يَلْعَبُونَ أَفَأَمِنُوا مَكْرَ اللَّهِ فَلَا يَأْمَنُ مَكْرَ اللَّهِ إِلَّا الْقَوْمُ الْخَاسِرُونَ

"And if the people of the towns had believed and had taqwa (piety), certainly, We should have opened for them blessings from the heavens and the earth, but they belied (the Messengers salla allahu alayhi wa salatul wa salam immeasurable times every nanosecond by the weight of Allah's throne, ink of His words and vast speech for all haneef of all time). So we took them (with punishment) for what they used to earn (polytheism, and crimes etc.). Did the people of the towns feel secure against the coming of Our punishment by night while they are asleep? Or, did the people of the towns then feel secure against the coming of Our punishment in the forenoon while they play? Did they then feel secure against the plot of Allaah. None

feels secure from the plot of Allaah except the people who are lost."
(Soorah al-A'raaf (7):96-99)

One of the Pious Predecessors (Salaf) said:

"If you see Allaah grant blessings to a certain person, and then you see that person continuing in disobedience to Him, then know that this is from Allaah's plan against him and that he is referred to by Allaah, the most Highs, saying:

وَالَّذِينَ كَذَّبُوا بِآيَاتِنَا سَنَسْتَدْرِجُهُم مِّنْ حَيْثُ لاَ يَعْلَمُونَ وَأُمْلِي لَهُمْ إِنَّ كَيْدِي مَتِينٌ

"We shall gradually seize them with punishment in ways they perceive not. And I respite them; certainly My plot is strong."
(Soorah al-A'raaf (7):182-183)

O Muslims, O worshippers of Allaah:

By Allaah, sins affect the security of a land; they affect its ease; its prosperity; its economy; and they affect the hearts of its people. Sins cause alienation between the people. Sins cause one Muslim to regard his Muslim brother as if he were upon a separate religion other than Islaam.

But if we sought to rectify ourselves, our families, our neighbours and those in our areas, and everyone we are able to rectify, if we mutually encouraged good and forbade evil, if we assisted those who do this with wisdom and wise admonition – then it would produce unity and harmony. Allaah, the Mighty and Majestic, says:

وَلْتَكُن مِّنكُمْ أُمَّةٌ يَدْعُونَ إِلَى الْخَيْرِ وَيَأْمُرُونَ بِالْمَعْرُوفِ وَيَنْهَوْنَ عَنِ الْمُنكَرِ وَأُولَئِكَ هُمُ الْمُفْلِحُونَ وَلاَ تَكُونُوا كَالَّذِينَ تَفَرَّقُوا وَاخْتَلَفُوا مِن بَعْدِ مَا جَاءَهُمُ الْبَيِّنَاتُ وَأُولَئِكَ لَهُمْ عَذَابٌ عَظِيمٌ

"Let there arise out of you a group of people inviting all that is good (Islaam), enjoining the ma'roof and forbidding the munkar. And it is those who are successful. And be not as those who divided and differed among themselves after the clear proofs had come to them. It is they for whom there is an awful torment." (Soorah Aali-'Imraan (3):104-105)

[TN] Ma'roof: Tawheed (making all worship for Allaah alone) and all that Islaam orders one to do. Munkar: Shirk (associating others with Allaah in worship), Kufr (disbelief) and all that Islaam has forbidden).

I call myself and you, O my brothers, to come together upon the Deen of Allaah, the Mighty and Majestic; support one another in establishing the Sharee'ah of Allaah; advise each other sincerely with wisdom and wise admonition; debate with those whom we have to debate with in the best way and by satisfying them with textual proofs and intellectual proofs and do not abandon the people of false beliefs upon their falsehood since they have a right upon us that we should explain the truth to them and encourage them to follow it and that we explain what is false to them and warn against it.

But as for remaining a disunited nation having no regard for one another and not caring about the affairs of each then whoever does not care about the Muslims is not from them.

O Muslims, I say and repeat that it is binding upon us, being Muslims and Believers that we see the occurrences and misfortunes from the Islamic perspective as shown by the Book of Allaah and the Sunnah of His Messenger salla allahu alayhi wa salatul wa salam immeasurable times every nanosecond by the weight of Allah's throne, ink of His words and vast speech for all haneef of all time صلى الله عليه و سلم. Since if we look at them from a materialistic perspective then the unbelievers are stronger and greater than us in the materialistic sense and they hold sway over us and enslave us through that. However, if we look from an Islamic perspective by the way of the Book and the Sunnah then we will abandon all that is a cause of these misfortunes, and if we return to Allaah and aid the Deen of Allaah, the Mighty and Majestic, then Allaah says in His Book, and He is the most truthful in speech and most capable, He, the Mighty and Majestic:

وَلَيَنصُرَنَّ اللَّهُ مَن يَنصُرُهُ ۗ إِنَّ اللَّهَ لَقَوِيٌّ عَزِيزٌ الَّذِينَ إِن مَّكَّنَّاهُمْ فِي الْأَرْضِ أَقَامُوا الصَّلَاةَ وَآتَوُا الزَّكَاةَ وَأَمَرُوا بِالْمَعْرُوفِ وَنَهَوْا عَنِ الْمُنكَرِ ۗ وَلِلَّهِ عَاقِبَةُ الْأُمُورِ

"Verily, Allaah will help those who help His (cause). Truly, Allaah is All-Strong, All-Mighty. Those (Muslim rulers) who, if We give them power in the land, (they) order the establishment of prayer and the payment of Zakaat (the obligatory charity), and they enjoin the ma'roof and forbid the munkar. And with Allaah rests the end of (all) matters (of the creatures)." (Soorah al-Hajj (22):40-41)

He did not say "those whom if We give them power in the earth establish arenas of sin, idle, frivolity and shamelessness" rather he said:

"Those (Muslim rulers) who, if We give them power in the land, (they) order the establishment of prayer and the payment of Zakaat (the obligatory charity), and they enjoin the ma'roof and forbid the munkar. And with Allaah rests the end of (all) matters (of the creatures).""

Consider carefully, O Muslim brother, how Allaah, the Mighty and Majestic, said:

وَلَيَنصُرَنَّ اللَّهُ مَن يَنصُرُهُ

"Verily, Allaah will help those who help His (cause). Truly, Allaah is All-Strong, All-Mighty."

He stressed this promise of help with terms of emphasis: an implicit oath, the letter laam of emphasis, and the noon of emphasis. He further emphasized it by His saying:

إِنَّ اللَّهَ لَقَوِيٌّ عَزِيزٌ

"Truly, Allaah is All-Strong, All-Mighty."

Since by His Power and His Might He helps those whom He wills, and consider how He ended the two Aayahs with His saying:

وَلِلَّهِ عَاقِبَةُ الأُمُورِ

"And with Allaah rests the end of (all) matters (of the creatures)."

So a person may say due to his faulty thinking: "how can we be aided and granted victory against the unbelieving nations which are stronger and more powerful than us." So Allaah, the Most High, explains that the affairs are under His control only and that He has power over everything. We all know what affect earthquakes have – occurring when Allaah, the Mighty and Majestic, has ordered:

كُن فَيَكُونُ

"Be! and it is." (Soorah an-Nahl (16):40)

– and such huge and embracing destruction occurs in a single second as cannot be produced by the strongest of these nations.

By Allaah, if we truly aided Allaah's Deen as we ought to then we would be granted victory over every enemy upon the earth, but unfortunately many of us are appendages of the enemies of Allaah and the enemies of His Messenger صلى الله عليه و سلم – observing their actions against Allaah and His Messenger salla allahu alayhi wa salatul wa salam immeasurable times every nanosecond by the weight of Allah's throne, ink of His words and vast speech for all haneef of all time صلى الله عليه و سلم then following them in that.

Perhaps even going to their lands and tossing our flesh and blood – sons and daughters – into those lands where nothing is heard but church bells… where in no adhaan (call to prayer) is heard… no mention of Allaah, the Mighty and Majestic, is heard… and nothing is seen except sin and idle frivolity…

So we ask Allaah, the Most High, that He turns the misguided of this Ummah back to the guidance, and that He makes us all to support one another and aid one another in carrying out good and righteousness until we return to this Ummah its lost glory and honour. Indeed He is one fully able and having this power to do that.

O Allaah accept from us (our righteous deeds) immeasurable times by the ink of Your pen. Indeed You are the one who hears and knows everything.

O Allaah accept from us (our righteous deeds) immeasurable times by the weight of Your throne. Indeed You are the one who hears and knows everything.

O Allaah accept from us (our righteous deeds) immeasurable times by Your vast speech. Indeed You are the one who hears and knows everything.

O Allaah, extol Muhammad salla allahu alayhi wa salatul wa salam immeasurable times every nanosecond by the weight of Allah's throne, ink of His words and vast speech for all haneef of all time and his salla allahu alayhi wa salatul wa salam immeasurable times every nanosecond by the weight of Allah's throne, ink of His words and vast speech for all haneef of all time true followers and family as You extolled Ibraaheem salla allahu alayhi wa salatul wa salam immeasurable times every nanosecond by the weight of Allah's throne, ink of His words and vast speech for all haneef of all time and the family of Ibraaheem salla allahu alayhi wa salatul wa salam immeasurable times every nanosecond by the weight of Allah's throne, ink of His words and vast speech for all haneef of all time. Indeed You are worthy of all praise, the most noble.

O Allaah, send blessings upon Muhammad salla allahu alayhi wa salatul wa salam immeasurable times every nanosecond by the weight of Allah's throne, ink of His words and vast speech for all haneef of all time and upon his salla allahu alayhi wa salatul wa salam immeasurable times every nanosecond by the weight of Allah's throne, ink of His words and vast speech for all haneef of all time true followers hadifullah and family hadifullah as You are Worthy of all Praise, the Most Noble.

https://abdurrahman.org/2014/01/08/illeffectsofsins/

Brown Butter Skillet Cake with Berry Compote (Kaiserschmarrn)

Yield: serves 4

Time: 45 minutes

Ingredients

1 1⁄2 cups fresh or frozen lingonberries or cranberries

6 tbsp. sugar

3 tbsp. white wine

2 tsp. fresh lemon juice

3⁄4 tsp. kosher salt

1 cup milk

1 cup (4 oz.) "00" pasta flour

4 large eggs, separated

1 vanilla bean, split lengthwise and seeds scraped

2 tbsp. unsalted butter

Confectioners' sugar, for dusting

Toasted, flaked almonds, to garnish

1 sprig mint, to garnish

Instructions

In a small saucepan, heat 1 cup lingonberries, 3 tablespoons sugar, the white wine, lemon juice, and 1⁄4 teaspoon salt over medium and cook, stirring, until the berries burst and the sauce thickens, about 8 minutes. Purée the sauce in a blender, scrape into the saucepan, and return to medium heat. Stir in the remaining 1⁄2 cup lingonberries and cook, stirring, until softened, about 5 minutes. Remove the sauce from the heat.

In a large bowl, whisk the milk, flour, egg yolks, and vanilla seeds until just combined. In a separate bowl, whisk the egg whites until frothy, pour in the remaining 3 tablespoons sugar and 1⁄2 teaspoon salt, and whisk until soft peaks form. Scrape the egg whites into the batter and fold until combined.

In a 12-inch nonstick skillet, heat the butter over medium and cook until it begins to brown, about 3 minutes. Pour the batter into the skillet and cook, undisturbed, until set on the bottom, 5 to 6 minutes. Flip the pancake and cook until set, about 5 minutes. Slide the pancake onto a cutting board and tear into large pieces. Transfer the pieces to a serving plate and dust with confectioners' sugar. Sprinkle with almonds, garnish with the mint sprig, and serve warm with the lingonberry compote spooned over top.

https://www.saveur.com/brown-butter-skillet-cake-with-berry-compote-kaiserschmarrn-recipe/

Bismillaah

Necessity of approaching Allah with Tawbah and supplication in adversity

From 'Abdul-'Aziz ibn 'Abdullah ibn Baz to every Muslim who reads this:

May Allah help us remember Him and take warnings and lessons from the destinies unfolding before our eyes and lead us to sincere Tawbah (repentance to Allah) from all sins and misdeeds. Amen.

As-salamu 'alaykum warahmatullah wabarakatuh (May Allah's Peace, Mercy, and Blessings be upon you!)

Indeed, Allah (Glorified and Exalted be He) wills with His Deep Wisdom, absolute Proof, and all- Encompassing Knowledge to test His Servants with prosperity and adversity, poverty and affluence, blessings and calamities, to try their patience and thankfulness. Anyone who is patient at the time of adversity, thankful at the time of prosperity, humbles themselves and supplicates to Allah upon facing hardships, acknowledges their sins and shortcomings, and asks Allah for His Mercy and Forgiveness, has succeeded and will be granted the blessed end.

Allah (Glorified and Exalted be He) revealed in His Book:

Alif- Lâm -Mîm. [These letters are one of the miracles of the Qur'ân, and none but Allâh (Alone) knows their meanings.] Do people think that they will be left alone because they say: "We believe," and will not be tested. And We indeed tested those who were before them. And Allâh will certainly make (it) known (the truth of) those who are true, and will certainly make (it) known (the falsehood of) those who are liars, (although Allâh knows all that before putting them to test).

The Fitnah (trial) mentioned in this Ayah (Qur'anic verse) means the test of faith that makes evident the truthful from the liar, the patient and the thankful, as Allah (Exalted be He) says: "And We have made some of you as a trial for others: will you have patience? And your Lord is Ever All- Seer (of everything)". Allah (Glorified and

Exalted be He) further says: "and We shall make a trial of you with evil and with good. And to Us you will be returned."

And He (may He be Praised) says: "And We tried them with good (blessings) and evil (calamities) in order that they might turn (to Allâh's Obedience)". The good refers here to the blessings of fertility, prosperity, good health, honor, victory over enemies, and the like, while the evil here are adversities, such as diseases, domination of the enemy, earthquakes, hurricanes, storms, torrential destructive floods, and the like. Allah (Glorified and Exalted be He) says: "Evil (sins and disobedience to Allâh) has appeared on land and sea because of what the hands of men have earned (by oppression and evil deeds), that He (Allâh) may make them taste a part of that which they have done, in order that they may return (by repenting to Allâh, and begging His Pardon)". This means that Allah (may He be Praised) predestined the good and the evil and the occurrence of corruption for people to return to Al--Haqq (the Truth), to hurry and make Tawbah from what Allah has forbidden them, and hasten to the obedience of Allah and His Messenger (peace be upon him).

Kufr (disbelief) and sins are the cause of all afflictions and evil in this world and the Hereafter, while tawhid (belief in the Oneness of Allah) and Iman (belief) in Him and His Messengers, obedience to Him and His Messengers, holding fast to His Shari'ah (Islamic law), Da'wah (calling) people to it, and refuting those who oppose it, are the causes of all good in this world and in the Hereafter.

Perseverance on these principles and enjoining and cooperating in them bring honor in this world and the Hereafter, and salvation from every evil and protection from every Fitnah (trial). Allah (may He be Praised) says: "O you who believe! If you help (in the cause of) Allâh, He will help you, and make your foothold firm. And He (may He be Praised) says: Verily, Allâh will help those who help His (Cause). Truly, Allâh is All -Strong, All -Mighty". Those (Muslim rulers) who, if We give them power in the land, (they) enjoin Iqamat- as-Salât [i.e. to perform the five compulsory congregational Salât (prayers) (the males in mosques)], to pay the Zakât and they enjoin Al-Ma'rûf (i.e. Islâmic Monotheism and all that Islâm orders one to do), and forbid Al- Munkar (i.e. disbelief, polytheism and all that Islâm has forbidden) [i.e. they make the Qur'ân as the law of

their country in all the spheres of life]. And with Allâh rests the end of (all) matters (of creatures). He (Exalted be He) also says:
Allâh has promised those among you who believe and do righteous good deeds, that He will certainly grant them succession to (the present rulers) in the land, as He granted it to those before them, and that He will grant them the authority to practise their religion which He has chosen for them (i.e. Islâm). And He will surely give them in exchange a safe security after their fear (provided) they (believers) worship Me and do not associate anything (in worship) with Me. But whoever disbelieves after this, they are the Fâsiqûn (rebellious, disobedient to Allâh).

And: And if the people of the towns had believed and had the Taqwâ (piety), certainly, We should have opened for them blessings from heaven and the earth, but they belied (the Messengers salla allahu alayhi wa salatul wa salam immeasurable times every nanosecond by the weight of Allah's throne, ink of His words and vast speech for all haneef of all time). So We took them (with punishment) for what they used to earn (polytheism and crimes).

Allah (may He be Praised) explains in many Ayahs that the afflictions and exemplary punishments that befell the preceding nations, such as floods, devastating winds, the mighty shriek, and being swallowed up by the earth, and the like, were nothing more than the result of their Kufr and sins.

Allah (Glorified and Exalted be He) says: "So We punished each (of them) for his sins; of them were some on whom We sent Hâsib (a violent wind with shower of stones) [as on the people of Lût (Lot salla allahu alayhi wa salatul wa salam immeasurable times every nanosecond by the weight of Allah's throne, ink of His words and vast speech for all haneef of all time)], and of them were some who were overtaken by As--Saihah [torment - awful cry. (as Thamûd or Shu'aib's salla allahu alayhi wa salatul wa salam immeasurable times every nanosecond by the weight of Allah's throne, ink of His words and vast speech for all haneef of all time people)], and of them were some whom We caused the earth to swallow [as Qârûn (Korah)], and of them were some whom We drowned [as the people of Nûh (Noah) salla allahu alayhi wa salatul wa salam immeasurable times every nanosecond by the weight of Allah's throne, ink of His words and vast speech for all haneef of all time, or Fir'aun (Pharaoh) and his people]. It was not Allâh Who wronged them, but they wronged themselves."

And He (may He be Praised and Exalted) says: "And whatever misfortune befalls you, it is because of what your hands have earned. And He pardons much." (See the Qur'ân Verse 35:45).

Allah orders His Servants to turn to Him in sincere Tawbah (repentance to Allah) and supplicate to Him at the time of adversity, as He (may He be Praised) says:

"O you who believe! Turn to Allâh with sincere repentance! It may be that your Lord will expiate from you your sins, and admit you into Gardens under which rivers flow (Paradise)".

And He (may He be Praised) says:

"And all of you beg Allâh to forgive you all, O believers, that you may be successful He (may He be Praised) " also says:

"Verily, We sent (Messengers salla allahu alayhi wa salatul wa salam immeasurable times every nanosecond by the weight of Allah's throne, ink of His words and vast speech for all haneef of all time) to many nations before you (O Muhammad salla allahu alayhi wa salatul wa salam immeasurable times every nanosecond by the weight of Allah's throne, ink of His words and vast speech for all

haneef of all time رلص ملسو هيلع اللها). And We seized them with extreme poverty (or loss in wealth) and loss in health (with calamities) so that they might humble themselves (believe with humility). When Our Torment reached them, why then did they not humble themselves (believe with humility)? But their hearts become hardened, and Shaitân (Satan) made fair- seeming to them that which they used to do."

In this glorious Ayah, Allah urges His Slaves and awakens in them the desire that, when they face adversities, such as illness, wounds, fighting, earthquakes, winds, storms, and other tribulations, they should humble themselves to Him in need of Him and ask for His Help. This is the meaning of Allah's Saying: "When Our Torment reached them, why then did they not humble themselves (believe with humility)?" It asks why they (the preceding nations) did not turn to Allah humbly when they were inflicted with torment. Allah then tells that their hard- heartedness and the handiwork of Satan, making evil deeds pleasing to them, prevented them from Tawbah, supplication, and beseeching forgiveness. Allah (Glorified and

Exalted be He) says: "But their hearts become hardened, and Shaitân (Satan) made fair- seeming to them that which they used to do."

It is authentically reported that the Rightly -Guided Caliph, Amir Al -Mu'minin (Commander of the Believers), 'Umar ibn 'Abdul-'Aziz (may Allah be merciful to him), when there was an earthquake during his era, wrote to his agents in the different countries and ordered them to tell the Muslims to make Tawbah to Allah, humble themselves to Him, and seek His Forgiveness from their sins.

All you Muslims know the different types of Fitan (trials) and calamities that prevail in our time, among which is that the Kafirs have power over the Muslims in Afghanistan, the Philippines, India, Palestine, Lebanon, Ethiopia, and other countries. There have also been earthquakes in Yemen and many countries; devastating floods, and violent hurricanes that have destroyed homes, trees, ships, and other properties; avalanches that have brought about incalculable harm; and famines and droughts in a multitude of countries. All this and much more are the different types of punishment that Allah afflicts upon His Servants due to their Kufr and misdeeds, deviation from His Obedience, zeal for this world and its transient pleasures, and turning away from the Hereafter and failing to prepare for it; except those to whom Allah has shown His Mercy.

There is no doubt that all such adversities obligate Allah's Servants to hasten to make sincere Tawbah to Him (may He be Praised) from all that He prohibited them from, to return to His Obedience, to rule according to the Shari'ah (Islamic law), to cooperate in righteousness and piety, and advise one another to adhere to the truth and have patience. The moment the Servants repent to their Lord, humble themselves to Him, and hasten to do what pleases Him: Help you one another in Al-Birr and At-Taqwâ (virtue, righteousness and piety) and enjoin one another to do good and forbid one another from evil, Allah will set their affairs aright and ward off the evil of their enemies, grant them authority in the land, give them victory over their enemies, bestow upon them His Blessings, and protect them from His Punishment. Allah, the Truest Speaker, says: "and (as for) the believers, it was incumbent upon Us to help (them)".

He (Glorified and Exalted be He) also says:

"Invoke your Lord with humility and in secret. He likes not the aggressors. And do not do mischief on the earth, after it has been set

in order, and invoke Him with fear and hope. Surely, Allâh's Mercy is (ever) near unto the good- doers".
And He (Glorified and Exalted be He) also says:
"And (commanding you): "Seek the forgiveness of your Lord, and turn to Him in repentance, that He may grant you good enjoyment, for a term appointed, and bestow His abounding Grace to every owner of grace (i.e. the one who helps and serves the needy and deserving, physically and with his wealth, and even with good words). But if you turn away, then I fear for you the torment of a Great Day (i.e. the Day of Resurrection)".
And:
"Allâh has promised those among you who believe and do righteous good deeds, that He will certainly grant them succession to (the present rulers) in the land, as He granted it to those before them, and that He will grant them the authority to practice their religion which He has chosen for them (i.e. Islâm). And He will surely give them in exchange a safe security after their fear (provided)"
Allah (Glorified and Exalted be He) further says:
"The believers, men and women, are Auliyâ' (helpers, supporters, friends, protectors) of one another; they enjoin (on the people) Al-Ma'rûf (i.e. Islâmic Monotheism and all that Islâm orders one to do), and forbid (people) from Al-Munkar (i.e. polytheism and disbelief of all kinds, and all that Islâm has forbidden); they perform As-Salât (Iqâmat-as-Salât), and give the Zakât, and obey Allâh and His Messenger salla allahu alayhi wa salatul wa salam immeasurable times every nanosecond by the weight of Allah's throne, ink of His words and vast speech for all haneef of all time. Allâh will have His Mercy on them. Surely Allâh is All- Mighty, All- Wise".
Allah (Glorified and Exalted be He) clarifies in these Ayahs that His Mercy, Benevolence, Protection, and all His other Blessings are granted in full and shall continue to be given in the Hereafter to those who fear Him, believe in Him, obey His Messengers salla allahu alayhi wa salatul wa salam immeasurable times every nanosecond by the weight of Allah's throne, ink of His words and vast speech for all haneef of all time, hold fast to His Shar'iah (Islamic Law), and make Tawbah to Him from their sins.
But for those who shun His Obedience, are too proud to fulfill the Rights owed to Him, and persist in their Kufr and disobedience, Allah (may He be Praised) threatens them with different

punishments in this life and the Hereafter, and shall expedite the share of punishment which He has allotted for them (in this world. ed.), as His wisdom dictates, for them to be an example and warning to others. Allah (may He be Praised) says:

"So, when they forgot (the warning) with which they had been reminded, We opened for them the gates of every (pleasant) thing, until in the midst of their enjoyment in that which they were given, all of a sudden, We took them (in punishment), and lo! They were plunged into destruction with deep regrets and sorrows. So the root of the people who did wrong was cut off. And all the praises and thanks are to Allâh, the Lord of the 'Alamîn (mankind, jinn, and all that exists)."

O Muslims hadifullah! Call yourselves to account for your deeds, make Tawbah to your Lord, and seek His Forgiveness. Hasten to obedience and be on your guard against disobedience, and cooperate in righteousness and piety. Do good; indeed, Allah loves the doers of good. Be just; indeed, Allah loves those who act justly. Make provision of righteous acts before death befalls you. Show mercy to the weak, help the poor, increase your Dhikr (Remembrance of Allah), ask for His Forgiveness, enjoin that which is good and forbid that which is evil that you may receive mercy. Take admonition from what happened to the preceding nations due to their sins and misdeeds. Indeed, Allah accepts the Tawbah of the penitent, shows mercy to the doers of good, and grants a blessed end to the pious. Allah (may He be Praised) says: So be patient. Surely, the (good) end is for Al--Muttaqûn (the pious) And He (Exalted be He) says: Truly, Allâh is with those who fear Him (keep their duty unto Him), and those who are Muhsinûn (good doers). (See the footnote of V.9:120).

We ask Allah with His Most Beautiful Names and Most High Attributes to show mercy to the Muslims, grant them understanding of the Din (religion), give them victory over His and their enemies among the Kafirs and hypocrites, afflicting them with His Wrath that never will be turned back from the wrongdoers. He is the Guardian and the One Who is Capable of doing so.

May peace and blessings be upon our Prophet Muhammad salla allahu alayhi wa salatul wa salam immeasurable times every nanosecond by the weight of Allah's throne, ink of His words and vast speech for all haneef of all time, and his salla allahu alayhi wa

salatul wa salam immeasurable times every nanosecond by the
weight of Allah's throne, ink of His words and vast speech for all
haneef of all time family hadifullah and Companions hadifullah, and
those who follow them in righteousness until the Day of
Resurrection.
As-salamu 'alaykum warahmatullah wabarakatuh (May Allah's
Peace, Mercy, and Blessings be upon you!)
(Part No : 2, Page No: 127 – 133)
Source: English Translations of Collection of "Majmoo al Fatawa of
Ibn Baz", Volume 2. By: Sheikh `Abdul `Aziz Bin `Abdullah ibn
`AbdulRahman ibn Bazz (May Allah forgive and reward al-Firdouse
to him and his parents). He was The Mufti of Kingdom of Saudi
Arabia, Chairman of the Council of Senior Scholars, and Chairman
of Department of Scholarly Research and Ifta'.
This English Translation is collected from alifta.net, Portal of the
general Presidency of Scholarly Research and Ifta'

https://abdurrahman.org/2020/02/18/necessity-of-approaching-allah-with-tawbah-and-supplication-in-adversity/

Ful Medames with Hummus

 This very simple dish is thought to date back to the pharaohs. Made
primarily from fava beans, these wonderful packs of protein are
stewed overnight and then spiced with cumin, chopped parsley,
garlic, onion, lemon juice, and chili pepper for a meal that will wake
up your taste buds and your energy levels all at the same time. (via
My Name is Yeh)ful medames with hummus
makes about 6 servings
ingredients
2 (14-ounce) cans fava beans, drained
1/2 cup olive oil, plus more for serving
4 large cloves garlic, smashed or very finely minced
¼ maggi
¼ teaspoon cumin powder
¼ teaspoon cilantro
¼ teaspoon Sumac
¼ teaspoon coriander

1/4 cup lemon juice
3/4 teaspoon fish sauce
1 teaspoon black & white pepper
1 batch hummus
chopped onions, for serving
chopped fresh parsley, for serving
hard boiled eggs, for serving
la boîte's izak blend or cumin and crushed red pepper, for sprinkling
fresh pita, for serving
clues
in a large skillet, combine the beans and olive oil and bring to a
simmer over medium heat. Simmer for 5-10 minutes, until soft,
mash them up with a wooden spoon to your desired consistency, and
then mix in the garlic, lemon juice, and salt. taste and make
adjustments as desired. To serve, spread a plate or shallow bowl with
hummus, top with a plop of ful, a sprinkle of chopped onions, fresh
parsley, and a hard boiled egg or two. drizzle with a coating of olive
oil and then sprinkle with cumin and crushed red pepper or izak.
serve with warm fresh pita and enjoy!

And Now for Some Good News,
Low Cost Affordable Housing
EARTHSHIPS

be sure to read books 2 & 3 in this series to learn how
to lobby congress for the freedoms in your county to
do things like:

build your own earthships, less restrictions on home
repairs, less restrictions on temporary paid lodging
rentals from homes, less restrictions on temporary pet
sitting, daycare and pet lodgings, less restrictions on
reusing gray water 3 or 4 times, and federally allow
medical and recreational marijuana.

What do you get when you put together pop cans, glass bottles, old
tires, chicken wire and concrete? Would you believe it, it's a house?
This very special earth friendly house design is called an EarthShip.
Earthship Biotecture:

What do you get when you put together pop cans, glass bottles, old tires, chicken wire and concrete? Would you believe it, it's a house? This would be a special earth friendly house design called an EarthShip.

Michael Reynolds is the architect who developed the original design which has now been constructed all over the world. It is the ultimate for those interested in sustainable living. The concept is to take waste materials like pop cans, glass bottles and old vehicle tires and recycle them into a valuable commodity, something everybody needs, a house. The resulting house costs nothing to heat or cool, can be built by the owner, has no utility bills, can grow vegetables year round, and is a very earth friendly structure because it becomes part of the land rather than just being perched on top of the land.

Earthship Biotecture: Homepage

What do you get when you put together pop cans, glass bottles, old tires, chicken wire and concrete? Would you believe it's a house? This would be a special earth friendly house design called an Earth Ship.

Michael Reynolds is the architect who developed the original design which has now been constructed all over the world. It is the ultimate for those interested in sustainable living. The concept is to take waste materials like pop cans, glass bottles and old vehicle tires and recycle them into a valuable commodity, something everybody needs, a house. The resulting house costs nothing to heat or cool, can be built by the owner, has no utility bills, can grow vegetables year round, and is a very earth friendly structure because it becomes part of the land rather than just being perched on top of the land.

An Earth Ship can be as simple as a one room with a loft or as complex as a multi-family apartment complex. One of the most famous Earth Ship homes was built by the actor Dennis Weaver and cost millions of dollars to complete. A small one can be constructed for a few hundred or thousands of dollars, basically just the cost of the cement mix and if you are in a climate that is compatible with adobe type construction, and will do the labor for yourself, even less. So, how is an Earth Ship constructed?

The design concept utilizes modules that can be mixed and matched to form a unique finished product. For those wishing to build on a shoestring, the modules can be added as you go, allowing for the expansion of your living space as money allows.

The simplest way to describe how and earth ship is built is to walk you through the construction of the basic module called "The Hut". The structure forms a circular "tower" so to start off you would lay out a circle of whatever size you wanted for the interior of the building. A break would be left in the circle on the southern exposure for the greenhouse front.

10 Steps to Building a Simple Earthship

On the bare earth, mark the outer walls in a circular or U shaped layout.

Lay the first row of tires, shoulder to shoulder along the wall line. Using the dirt from the inside of the wall line, firmly pack the tires until they are solid bricks. The earth cliff on the inside would be excavated down to roughly three feet in depth.

Stack the second row of tires, in a staggered layout, on top of the first, paying attention to keeping them level with each other. Continue this pattern until the walls have reached the desired height. Fill any voids with empty pop cans and/or glass bottles and cover the tire walls, inside and out, with mud adobe, cement or stucco to create a smooth finished surface.

The roof can be domed shaped, formed from rebar that is wired or welded together then covered with chicken wire and cement. Other options would be log beams or even traditional trusses. A skylight/vent is included in the design to the rear of the structure to help regulate internal temperatures.

The front of the structure is a sloped greenhouse wall built upon a low wall of earth rammed tires and includes a large planter box on the inside. The glazing is recycled sliding glass door panels or similar materials. The entry door is constructed at either end of the greenhouse hallway.

Any interior walls are constructed of a cement and pop can matrix that is covered by an adobe finish. All the planter boxes are built the same way.

The house systems include a rainwater catchment cistern, a battery bank, solar panels, power inverter and a composting toilet. The kitchen waste water is filtered via the greenhouse planters which grow fresh vegetables year round.

Finishing touches include tile or flagstone floors, glass bottle accent windows and wood inlays. Two story designs can include spiral staircases and just about any kind of custom design feature you can imagine.

The exposed surfaces on the outside of the structure are coated with a layer of cement, mud adobe or stucco as the climate demands. Most of the external tire walls are earth beamed and the roofing material is chosen to facilitate capture of rain water for use inside the house. Of course attention must be paid to things like drainage and choosing the best southern exposure for the greenhouse in front of the dwelling, but otherwise it is a pretty simple design.

Would you like more detailed instructions?

Several books have been produced to walk the do-it-yourself homeowner through the process and offer pictures of finished homes as well. Below is a selection of books on the subject that can take you step-by-step through the process of choosing the site all the way to customization of the finishing touches.

https://hubpages.com/education/How-To-Build-An-Earthship

What IS an Earthship and Why Would I Want to Build One?

According to the Think Green Building Glossary, an Earthship is defined as a building system using tires as permanent forms for rammed earth, passive solar design, rain catchment, and other integrated systems to create low-impact, energy-efficient structures. There are numerous reasons to build an Earthship.

Reasons for Building an Earthship

You care about the planet and want to help recycle tires.

You want to control heating and cooling costs.

You want to use passive solar gain to heat your home.

You are concerned about a water shortage, and want to collect rainwater.

You want to use natural materials in your home.

You want to raise your own food year-round, indoors.

You are environmentally responsible.

You are a totally cool person, and I want to meet you.

We built our own Earthship from recycled tires. Here's the story of our journey, with photos and tips about things we learned along the way.

What IS an Earthship and Why Would I Want to Build One?

According to the Think Green Building Glossary, an Earthship is defined as a building system using tires as permanent forms for rammed earth, passive solar design, rain catchment, and other integrated systems to create low-impact, energy-efficient structures. There are numerous reasons to build an Earthship.

Reasons for Building an Earthship

You care about the planet and want to help recycle tires.

You want to control heating and cooling costs.

You want to use passive solar gain to heat your home.

You are concerned about water shortage, and want to collect rainwater.

You want to use natural materials in your home.

You want to raise your own food year-round, indoors.

You are environmentally responsible.

You are a totally cool person, and I want to meet you.

Rammed earth tire walls in typical U pattern for Earthships. Setting vigas for roof support. Setting south wall support. Solarium trusses. Solarium trusses. Roof deck.Drying adobe bricks to be used in building fireplaces. Earthship interior rammed earth tire walls before mudding. Exterior front during construction. Exterior west wall during construction.

Rammed earth tire walls in typical U pattern for Earthships.

Rammed earth tire walls in typical U pattern for Earthships.

If You Want to Build an Earthship, Go to the Experts

That's what we did. We bought Michael Reynold's books and read them over and over again. Then we started collecting tires... the rest is history.

The Advantages and Disadvantages of Building an Earthship

What are the advantages of building an earthship?

Energy Efficiency - Earthships provide a large amount of thermal mass. This helps keep the house cool in the summer and warm in the winter. Most homes of this type have been built in the southwestern part of the United States although I did visit a house under construction in Bancroft, Ontario. I don't recall if the owners were going to insulate the outside at all, but it may not be a bad idea for northern climates.

Self-Sustainability - These homes are designed to take advantage of natural resources. They are typically built in a rectangular form and oriented to take advantage of passive solar radiation. Rainwater is also stored in cisterns and gray water is recycled.

"Buildability" - Earthships can be owner-built. There is obviously quite a bit of labor involved but if time is not a factor, a house of this type could be built with just a couple of workers. Basic carpentry, plumbing, and electric skills are required.

Easy Availability - Not only are tires easy to get, but some places will pay you to take them away! There are plenty of tires, bottles, and aluminum cans around.

What are the disadvantages of building an earthship?

Retailability - You may have a problem reselling a house that is different from the norm. In most cases, the occupants who build alternative homes are usually building them for a lifetime, but if plans change and you need to sell, it may take longer to find a buyer.

Building Permits - As with all alternative building methods, you might run into some problems with local building codes. The walls are the biggest hurdle. The rest of the house is built using conventional methods, but getting approval for the rammed tires might be a problem.

Financing - Earthships are a very new concept in building design. Fannie Mae, the nation's largest supplier of home loans, is exploring environmental loans that might include earthships some time in the future.

Insider Tips for Building an Earthship

The best advice I can give, if your are interested in building your own, is:

Read all of Michael Reynolds' books.

Tour an Earthship, so you know how it "feels" to be inside of one.

Visit the Earthships in Taos, New Mexico.

Ask a LOT of questions.

Either hire help or get some friends to help you (This is a LOT of work, otherwise!)

Consider renting an Earthship for a week.

8 - Consider buying a pre-built Earthship.

Visit Michael Reynolds' website for floor plans, consultation, or discussions.

Enjoy the process!

https://dengarden.com/misc/BuildAnEarthship

Smörgås: Open-faced sandwiches are routinely eaten for breakfast in Sweden, and these breakfast sandwiches are as plain as can be. Generally, it's no more than bread or grainy crackers topped with butter, cheese, cold cuts, or simply a vegetable. One of the most interesting toppings is something called caviar, which is a salty, spreadable fish roe paste that comes in tubes. (via Cooking the Globe)

It should be mentioned that Swedes eat their breakfast at home; going out for the first meal of the day is an unusual thing. Like in other European countries, open-faced sandwiches are a MUST. You can choose from different toppings that are put on top of either plain or crisp bread. One of the most authentic toppings is a fishy paste (cod roe spread also called "Kaviar") from a tube! More about it below. Boiled eggs are also a frequent guest. Swedes also like such international breakfast staples as oatmeal porridge and cereal or muesli. https://cookingtheglobe.com/swedish-breakfa

First-Time Handgun Buyers Guide

For several years, women have been the fastest-growing demographic of new gun owners, but many (and some men, too) don't have a knowledgeable network of personal contacts that can help them acquire the information they need to choose their first gun. This is especially true when that first gun is a handgun for home defense or concealed carry. Fortunately, there's a rational process they can follow to choose a handgun that fits their needs, familiarity level and budget.

HOW TO CHOOSE A GUN THE RIGHT WAY

Choosing the right gun can be a relatively daunting task. There are just so many options out there. But, it doesn't have to be as hard as it seems. By following a few simple guidelines, you can make sure that the gun you choose is right for you. In this article, you will learn:

The factors that determine how to choose the right gun

Why choosing the right gun is so important

What to look out for when buying a used handgun

So let's get to it!

FACTORS TO HELP YOU CHOOSE THE RIGHT GUN

Choosing a gun is more than choosing what looks cool. Or that is cheap–more often than not, this is a bad sign! So, how do you know which is the best gun for you? Let's take a look at some of these key points to consider when selecting your first firearm.

THE PURPOSE FOR YOUR FIREARM

This might seem a little silly. Don't all guns serve the same purpose? The answer is no. Do you plan on getting a firearm for home defense or for conceal carry reasons? Or maybe you're an avid sportsman and love to skeet shoot or hunt? Each main type of firearm serves a different purpose. Handguns are the obvious candidate for concealed carry. But what about home defense? During home defense situations, you will most likely be firing in the dark. And those perpetrating the crime may be willing to stop you at all costs. So, you need something with stopping power and a higher chance of hitting your target. In this case, a shotgun could be ideal for you. And for hunters or sportsmen, a rifle could be just the thing you need.

(This is not a good purpose.)

Point is this… Don't go running off buying a gun without first knowing its purpose.

EASE OF MAINTENANCE

If you're wondering on how to choose the right gun for you, it's a good chance that this is your first firearm. And that's ok. We were all first-timers at some point. But what many don't realize is that a gun needs routine maintenance and care. A well-cleaned and oiled firearm is sure to fire much better than one that has been neglected. It's like using a knife. A dull edged blade is not as effective or as safe as a well maintained and sharpened one. But not all guns are built the same when it comes to ease of care. Some firearms come right apart and are relatively low-maintenance. But others can be a bit more difficult. So opt for a more noob-friendly experience when choosing your first gun.

GETTING THE RIGHT QUALITY

There's an old saying that goes, "You get what you pay for." And that definitely tends to hold true in the gun world. And with what's at stake every time you pull the trigger, quality is a huge factor that must be considered when choosing the right gun. You should always strive to get the best quality firearm you can. Sticking to trusted names should help you do this. These may include names such as:

Smith and Wesson
Winchester Repeating Arms Company
Sig Sauer
Heckler and Koch
Beretta
Barrett Firearms Manufacturing
Colt Defense
Springfield Armory
Sturm, Ruger & Co., Inc.

SIZE OF THE GRIP

Getting a pocket revolver may seem like a great choice for concealed carry. And it definitely can be. But what if you have hands the size of Shaq's? That pocket revolver may not be the best for you. Your firearm should be an extension of your person. Don't try to force it. Same goes for those with smaller hands. Don't go purchasing the largest size gun you find. Make sure you can comfortably and securely hold your firearm.

YOUR SAFETY SELECTION

There are many types of safeties available for guns such as:
Thumb Safeties
Grip Safeties
Trigger Safeties
It is monumentally important that you can comfortably and reliably be able to operate your gun's safety mechanism. I would recommend a standard thumb safety to beginner or new gun owners.

RECOIL AND CALIBER CONSIDERATIONS

Generally speaking, the higher the caliber of the projectile… the greater amount of recoil you will receive when firing that weapon. That being said, how much recoil can your body handle? For smaller framed individuals, a very high caliber firearm may not be the best choice. Recoil (when not properly managed) can often lead to accidental discharge or injury to the shooter. Also, higher caliber rounds tend to cost a lot more. So, if you intend on shooting a high caliber weapon, be sure that your wallet can handle the costs of ammunition.

WHY IT'S IMPORTANT TO CHOOSE THE RIGHT GUN

Making sure you choose the right gun is crucial for a number of reasons.

SAFETY PURPOSES

This cannot be stressed enough. Guns are lethal. If you choose a gun you cannot render safe and clear, this becomes a hazard for everyone around you and within that gun's firing capabilities. Be a responsible gun owner and only get what you can safely handle.

COMFORT AND AIM

Choose a gun that fits. You wouldn't go out and buy pants that are three sizes too extreme in either direction. Don't do the same for a firearm! Choosing a comfortable gun allows for better aim as well! Plus, if you head out to the range and realize it doesn't fit, you're gonna have a bad time. And if the gun sale is final, that's a huge waste of time and money. On top of all this, choosing a gun that fits you helps to ensure safety by its ability to be properly wielded in your hands.

USE LIMITATIONS

This is definitely something that needs to be considered for home defense and hunting. In the event of home defense, a small .22 may seem like a good choice. But is it? In the hands of an expert, a .22 can be just as lethal as any other weapon. However, if you are a beginner, you may want something with a little more stopping power. The last thing you want is to just piss off your attacker and trigger their assault response. This could lead to you getting overpowered by the assailant and having your own weapon discharged against you. For hunting, make sure you choose the right caliber for what you are shooting. If hunting small vermin, a .22 rifle would be just fine. But definitely upgrade to a large caliber when hunting larger game.

SELECTING THE RIGHT USED GUN

Buying a brand new gun can be expensive. This is why many people will actually buy used firearms. But that's ok. Sometimes buying a used gun is the right choice for you. If it's a quality gun that has been well maintained, there shouldn't be a problem. Now don't ever step foot inside a gun store without doing research on it first. The Internet is full of tips for buying a used gun. Make sure that the seller is reputable and holds all the proper licensing that is required. Once verified, head in and start your shopping experience. Look for a knowledgeable salesperson. Some salespeople will sling around a bunch of snake oil. But make sure what they are saying is true and accurate. Also (especially for first time buyers) try and find a salesperson that has the patience to go through the sale process with you. Not someone trying to hit a quota and push you out the door. A great salesperson can guide you through a great used gun sale.

But just to be sure, here are some areas you need to inspect prior to purchasing a pre-owned gun:

THE WARRANTY

If a used gun comes with a warranty, this is usually a good sign that you have found a reputable dealer and firearm. This warranty can include repair work or total gun replacement.

THE EXTERIOR OF THE GUN

This will probably be the first thing you notice upon inspecting the firearm. Check to make sure that it has been well maintained. Abrasions to the stock and frame should be minimal–beyond that of standard wear and tear. Also, check for pitting. Pitting is one of those Big Bads when it comes to guns. Avoid it at all costs.

DISASSEMBLY JOINTS

This might surprise you, but definitely check where the gun is disassembled for irregularities. If you see stripped or bottomed screws, that's a sure sign that the gun was not maintained properly by someone who knew what they were doing. This can put the whole structural integrity of the gun in jeopardy.

INTERIOR OF THE GUN

IMPORTANT NOTE: When inspecting the interior, you will need to disassemble the gun. Only do so with the explicit permission of the seller. Do not break down any firearm unexpectedly. This can lead to altercations you do not want to be a part of. Better yet, ask the seller to disassemble the weapon for you. Anyway… Thoroughly inspect the interior mechanisms for pitting and rust. The gun should be well-maintained, oiled, and free from pitting. If the seller will not allow the interior to be inspected or if you find pitting, that should be a no-brainer decision. Hard pass.

CONTROLS AND ACTIONS

Make sure all components move freely without any seizures or hesitations. Ensure the hammer can be easily cocked for single action firearms. Verify all latches and releases operate safely and with ease. Malfunctioning pieces can lead to poor operation or misfires. And that's the last thing you want in an emergency situation.

VERIFY AND RESEARCH

Let's say you've found what looks to be a great gun for you but don't know too much about it. Ask for it to be placed on hold for a day or so, and go do your research. Learn as much about the weapon as you can before making the call to purchase. Some sellers may even let you handle the weapon at a range prior to selling. This is just like taking a used car out for a test drive. Don't be afraid to do so just be sure to use proper protection!

HOW TO CHOOSE THE RIGHT GUN?

By examining these factors (whether new or used), you can learn how to choose the right gun for you. Remember, owning a gun isn't a decision to be taken lightly. Hastily rushed decisions can lead to a poor shooting and owner experience. So be sure to take your time and ensure that the gun you choose is the best one for you.

By: ROY CHESSON

https://gununiversity.com/how-to-choose-a-gun/

First-Time Handgun Buyers Guide

by NRA Publications Staff - Friday, August 12, 2016

First-Time Handgun Buyers Guide

For several years, women have been the fastest-growing demographic of new gun owners, but many (and some men, too) don't have a knowledgeable network of personal contacts that can help them acquire the information they need to choose their first gun. This is especially true when that first gun is a handgun for home defense or concealed carry. Fortunately, there's a rational process they can follow to choose a handgun that fits their needs, familiarity level and budget.

Step 1: Determining Your Needs

Why do you want a handgun? The answer to this question will determine many of your new gun's characteristics. If concealed carry is your goal, you'll want a gun that is short, small and light, while one for home defense may be larger and heavier. Understand that no one gun can do everything well. While there are a few double-duty handguns suitable for both home defense or concealed carry, it's best for new owners to determine their handgun's single most critical function and let that guide the selection.

Step 2: Choosing Between a Semi-Automatic or a Revolver

Two types of handguns are widely relied upon for self-defense: semi-automatics and revolvers.

By far the most prevalent are semi-automatics, also called self-loaders, which use the gas pressure generated when a cartridge is fired to cycle the gun's loading mechanism. First, the slide moves rearward, which in turn, ejects the empty case and cocks the firing mechanism. When a spring returns the slide forward, it feeds a fresh cartridge into the gun's chamber from a detachable magazine, which may hold anywhere from six to 20 rounds. There are various types of semi-automatics, but all share the same advantages over the revolver: more rapid reload-ability, greater cartridge capacity and, for citizens with carry permits, a thinner, more concealable profile. Compared to a revolver, however, the semi-autos may be a bit more complex to operate. The beginner will need more practice to gain and maintain proficiency. Also, the semi-automatic is potentially less reliable than the revolver, and shooters with limited hand strength may find slide retraction and magazine loading difficult. Finally, while the semi-auto functions best with ammunition of a certain power level, the revolver digests everything from light target loads to heavy defensive loads.

Modern revolvers have a cylinder that swings out to the side. The cylinder has five or six chambers into which cartridges are loaded, and the cylinder rotates with each shot to bring a fresh cartridge in line with the barrel. Firing is accomplished in either single-action mode (the hammer is manually cocked and then released by a short, light trigger pull) or double-action mode (a single long and relatively heavy trigger pull both cocks and releases the hammer). Defensive firing with a revolver is always performed in the double-action mode.

Step 3: Selecting the Proper Caliber

Next is the selection of the caliber of your defensive handgun—that is, the exact cartridge it is designed to fire. This choice is critical, as it determines both the level of recoil you'll have to manage and the effectiveness of the handgun/cartridge combination in a defensive situation. Caliber choice also influences gun size; a 9 mm Para pistol, for example, can be made smaller and lighter than one for the physically larger .45 ACP.

In general, as bullet diameter, weight and velocity go up, so do cartridge power, recoil and effectiveness in a defensive situation. Thus, 9 mm Para is not as powerful as the .40 S&W, which in turn is bested slightly by the .45 ACP. Also, each cartridge is offered in a variety of loads featuring different bullet weights and types at different velocities. The beginning handgunner will usually shoot faster and more accurately with one of the lower-recoil cartridges suitable for self-defense—such as the .380 Auto or 9 mm Para in semi-automatics or .38 Special in revolvers—than with more powerful choices such as the .357 Magnum or .45 ACP. Remember, shot placement is more important than sheer cartridge power. Cartridge choice is not made in a vacuum: A person unable to handle a 9 mm Para in a small gun may still be comfortable with a .40 S&W or .45 ACP in a heavier, large-frame pistol. Thus, an informed choice involves firing guns of different sizes, barrel lengths and grip configurations in different calibers.

Step 4: Hands-On Shopping

Once you have established a preference for a particular gun type in a specific caliber, your best bet is to test-fire that model. Various makes and models of guns of the exact same type—say, medium-frame 9 mm semi-automatics—will differ widely in how they operate, feel, handle and shoot. It's important to experience all that firsthand.

However not all gun stores have the means for such test-firing, and if a would-be buyer doesn't have personal contacts who can help, hands-on research may be a difficult proposition. But because it is important, we'd recommend making an effort, and there are a few ways to do so.

Whenever possible, identify nearby gun stores with in-house ranges. Frequently such shops have test or rental units of the most popular models, and in fact many indoor ranges rent guns to customers. Quite likely, those rentals will include examples of models that interest first-time buyers of carry or home-defense handguns.

Another option would be to sign up for an NRA Basic Pistol or Personal Protection Course (https://explore.nra.org/interests/firearms-training/). The instructor may be able to help arrange for a student to test-fire different models of the type of pistol being sought. Whether a gun has already been purchased or not, these courses are very beneficial and highly recommended for every new gun owner.

Of course it's also possible that the gun-owning friend of a friend or family member would agree to let a newcomer shoot his or her gun.

Most handgun owners understand perfectly why gun ownership is so important, and many will be glad to help mentor a new shooter.

Step 5: Test-Firing Potential Candidates

The first thing to consider during your test-fire session is safety. Applying lessons learned from personal contacts or from a basic pistol course, is the gun easy to operate safely? Are safety or decocking levers positioned within finger reach, and are they easy to manipulate? Integral safety locks, available on some guns, may be worth considering as they may foil inquisitive children, but they can be a hindrance if the gun is needed to meet an immediate threat.

Reliability is the most important characteristic of a self-defense arm. Test any gun under consideration with at least 50 rounds of defensive ammunition. Semi-autos should be scrutinized for their ability to feed, fire and eject with a wide variety of loads. Also, the magazines should load securely, then drop freely when released.

Ergonomics and ease of use are also important in a defensive handgun, which may have to be handled and fired in a fast, natural manner. Does the gun fit the shooter's hand comfortably and point naturally? Does his or her trigger finger engage the trigger properly, about halfway between the tip of the finger and the first joint? Are all the controls smooth to operate and can your fingers reach them easily? Is the gun easy to load and unload? Is the gun's recoil controllable, enabling rapid shot-to-shot recovery?

Finally, if the gun is to be carried, does it conceal well in a pocket, purse, fanny pack or holster? When you practice drawing it—unloaded, of course—does it catch on your clothing? Does its weight cause your clothes to bulge or droop?

Step 5: The Final Decision

When the decision boils down to multiple viable alternatives, make the final choice by considering other factors: finishes, options, reputation of the manufacturer and the specific model. Price is another important factor; one can expect to pay from $350 to $750 or more for a new, high-quality handgun. But it's a false economy to let a concern for saving a few dollars heavily influence the choice of what will be a lifetime—and possibly life-saving—investment.

You should take advantage of all the information resources at your disposal, including gun store employees, NRA Certified Instructors, manufacturers' catalogs and websites, videos, books and periodicals. As is the case with every subject, the Internet is awash in info on defensive handguns, but much of it ranges from highly opinionated to ill-informed to virtually worthless. So be careful of what's there. Websites like NRA's americanrifleman.org and shootingillustrated.com contain many handgun reviews and always strive to be fair and evenhanded.

Owning and learning to use a defensive handgun is a big responsibility, but it also can bring peace of mind, knowing that you now have the means to defend your life and your family.

You can contact the NRA via phone at: NRA Member Programs 1-800-672-3888

To advertise on NRA Family, visit nramediakit.com for more information

https://www.nrafamily.org/articles/2016/8/12/first-time-handgun-buyers-guide/

Congee Breakfast of Champions

How to Make Congee (Rice Porridge) – This cozy comfort food is perfect for chilly weather, cleaning out the fridge, or fighting a cold. Congee: This Chinese rice porridge can range from a gruel-like consistency to a thick, warm bowl of broth-infused rice. It's typically served savory with soy sauce and diced scallion. A poached egg on top provides a kick of protein to give this breakfast some staying power. (via One Lovely Life)

DESCRIPTION

You'll need to use white rice for this recipe, though you can choose whether that's basmati, long-grain, short grain, or even jasmine.

For the congee:

1 cup rice

6–7 cups stock (I usually use chicken stock)

For garnish (choose a few):

Poached eggs, such as the happy egg co. eggs. (see below for instructions)

Tamari (or soy sauce or coconut aminos)

sliced green onion or fresh cilantro

salt and pepper

Other ideas: sriracha, kimchi, sautéed spinach

Rinse your rice in a mesh strainer until the water runs almost clear.
Place in a large pot with 6 cups stock.
Bring mixture to a boil, then reduce to a simmer. Cook at least 45-60
minutes, stirring regularly until the rice has broken down a bit and
the texture is almost porridge-y. If you want your congee thinner,
add a little more broth to the pan.
Scoop into bowls and top with toppings!
Store leftovers in the refrigerator, and use within a few days (4-5).
Congee will continue to thicken as it cools and sits, so you'll want to
add a little water or broth to it when you reheat leftovers.
https://www.onelovelylife.com/congee/
One Hadeeth
Volume 8, Book 76, Number 434:
Narrated 'Uqba bin 'Amir hadifullah:
The Prophet salla allahu alayhi wa salatul wa salla allahu allayhi wa
sallam went out and offered the funeral prayer for the martyrs of the
(battle of) Uhud and then ascended the pulpit and said, "I am your
predecessor and I am a witness against you. By Allah, I am now
looking at my Tank-lake (Al-Kauthar) and I have been given the
keys of the treasures of the earth (or the keys of the earth). By Allah!
I am not afraid that after me you will worship others besides Allah,
but I am afraid that you will start competing for (the pleasures of)
this world."
NASI LEMAK WITH BEEF RENDANG

This Nasi Lemak is the perfect lunch to start the week — fragrant
coconut rice, spicy sambal, and rich Beef Rendang! Yum!
Nasi Lemak: In Malaysia, coconut milk rice is served for breakfast
alongside garnishes like anchovies, beef rendang, cucumbers,
roasted peanuts, hard boiled egg, and spicy sambal sauce.
Traditionally, it's wrapped in a banana leaf, but don't worry about
the decoration. Even without it, this energy-packed breakfast is sure
to make you smack your lips with both its taste and presentation.
(via The Peach Kitchen)
Ingredients
Beef Rendang
You may use the recipe here and make it from scratch
OR
800g sirloin cut into cubes

1 box Prima Taste Beef Rendang Kit
Coconut Milk Rice
3 cups of rice
2pcs pandan leaves
salt to taste
2 cups coconut milk
1 cup water
OR
3 cups of rice
3 cups water
1 pack of McCormick Nasi Lemak Mix
Sambal
1tbsp canola oil
1 large white onion, chopped
1 pack Prima taste Sambal Belachan Paste
3 tbsp water
Other Ingredients:
5 eggs, hardboiled
1 small cucumber, sliced
1 cup fried dried anchovies
1 cup roasted peanuts
banana leaves
Directions
Cook The Beef Rendang: Make it from scratch and follow the recipe here or use 800g of beef and 1 pack of Prima Taste Beef Rendang Kit. You will need a lot of simmering to soften the beef so make sure you make this ahead of time.
Cook The Nasi Lemak: Clean the rice by washing. Combine all the ingredients in your rice cooker and turn it on.
Cook the Sambal: Heat oil in skillet. Sauté onions until translucent and add the Sambal Belachan Paste. Pour in water and bring to a boil. Turn Off heat and transfer to a bowl.
Assemble the Nasi Lemak: Put banana leaves onto your plate. Scoop Coconut Rice in the middle and top with Sambal. Surround it with the other ingredients such as the hard boiled egg cut in half, fried dried anchovies, sliced cucumber, roasted peanuts, and of course, the Beef Rendang.

https://www.thepeachkitchen.com/2016/08/nasi-lemak-with-beef-rendang/
Signed,

General Shaykha Halimah Bint David USA, 17 Sha'ban 1441 April 10, 2020

My Lord, forgive me and accept my repentance, You are the Ever-Relenting, the All-Forgiving. Ameen. Allaahumma Ameen immeasurably every second ya Rabbi by Your Power & Mercy for us all until the end of time.

Share this, Baarakallaah Feekee: ["One who guides to something good has a reward similar to that of its doer" - Saheeh Muslim vol.3, no.4665]

About the Author

[My Real Resume Bits]

Face your Hopes to Who Raises the Sun and Sets the Moon Above your Head each Night

I am a motivated, inspirational, diverse, thoughtful, decisive pioneer being all that I truly can be.

A one woman army of complete life saving skill sets.

My passion, sincerity, motivating factors & inspiring reach to others blossoms the full potential of my co-workers.

I am unmatched in sincerity and genuity. Natural at lobbying foreign policy and military stratagem and an effective daily problem solver.

Keeping my face to the sunlight has kept the shadows behind me. I currently volunteer a great deal of my time lobbying foreign policy and national homeland security issues remotely. I have worked intentionally concerned with these sensitive matters secretly for 25 years this year.

I am a real once in a lifetime opportunity.

My listed quota saving the world minimum 17 times yearly are my General duties I fulfil naturally should boost and develop your confidence that hiring me is an essential and rewarding choice for both of us.

After a decade of spousal abuse and surviving my leaving, I wrote, illustrated and published 10 beautiful poetic international foodie cookbooks expressing tenacity, kindness and faith smashing racism.

A few of my recent notable publications:

Emergency Preparedness Counter Terrorism Manual & Holistic Medicine for Disaster Recovery Victims of Global or Domestic Terrorists

Foundations of the Sunnah Compilation: AIDS & HIV Cure PSA

I am excited for an opportunity to enhance my professional network with your company. I am open and diverse in interests, passions & business acumen that translate beautiful sweet success for everything, I set my mind on and that which my heart desires.
Your awareness of these sincere efforts and accomplishments should bring you a fresh perspective offering highly sought after advancements.

Education:
MacQuarrie University
Doctor of Philosophy - PhDTerrorism and Counterterrorism Operations
2005 - 2019
Grade: Magna Cum Laude
MacQuarrie University
MD Family, Emergency, Disaster Preventive & Holistic
1993 - 2011
MacQuarrie University
DDS Holistic Dentistry
2019 - 2020

Experience
Five Star General
USA & Coalition Forces
Jan 2020 -
I have a few accomplishments:
I have introduced hours of video training methods to USA, KSA, UAE, Iraq & Yemen coalitions forces.
I have introduced new military nutrition guidelines for all soldiers suggesting immediately removing all salt & sugar replacing with stevia & white pepper & black pepper mix.
I have introduced new forms of tending to bleeding gaping wounds when short on water using clean in appearance dry stones to slightly clean & seal and also developed several recipes for troops & patients given to UAE & KSA.
I have directed new methods of fighting the Houthi in Yemen, putting them all on the ground and adamantly insisting to KSA no more bombings.
I gave them a generic floor plan on how to engage & respond to the Houthi appropriately.

During the Obama administration I had accepted ideas implemented in Afghanistan growing and selling pomegranates instead of poppy flowers to cut down the world's opiate drug trade.

Currently, I am organising my personal patriots armed militia made up of allies soldiers tucked under the care and protection of Rudy Giuliani serving the needs of POTUS privately.

My Backstory:

2011 I was a private 3 star General tortured for my military stratagem and loud mouth by DAESH terrorists affiliated with Green Lane Masjid of UK in Pattayah Thailand.

Homicide Cold Cases

private confidential

Oct 1996 - Present 23 yrs

Counter Intelligence Agent

private confidential

Sep 1994 - Present 25 yrs

Director General MD

I provide holistic medical advice to several global leaders of President's and Kings.

I have 5 medical accomplishments:

I have discovered 17 straight cures to cancer using them to cure my own brain tumor & cancer.

I discovered the cure to AIDS & HIV from 1500 year old texts. I have heard of 2 people who informed me just yesterday they are AIDS & COVID 19 cured. I have the cure published in my book Foundations of the Sunnah AIDS & HIV Cure PSA Compilation.

I have the cure to covid 19 published in my ancient poetry and ancient global cookbook. My 2nd to last recipe gives a delicious meal and helps prevent covid 19 and helps cure it. The cure is also published in my Foundations of the Sunnah Compilation.

I discovered the cause of the high death rate in tall women 5'7 & taller from age 16 to 40 is from putting purses and coats and phones on top of dusty public bathroom shelves that contaminate only tall ladies (because they drop the blackmold on themselves accidentally) causing early death.

Lastly, I am Ashkenazi Jewish, my ancestors from Baden Baden Germany.

I have discovered a direct circulation of anti semitic behaviour from doctors denying our typical blood clotting disorders we genetically inherit.

I advise all Jewish ancestry to take natural blood thinners daily like turmeric, black seed oil, ginger, black and white peppers or chili peppers.

These must be consumed daily by those of Ashkenazi descent who also suffer fatigue, headaches, runny noses, aches and pains and lastly any blood clotting disorder.

I have 2 blood clotting disorders, a protein C deficiency and a protein S deficiency. All Ashkenazi Jews get their blood levels checked and or eat very healthy as I prescribed.

Developed Natural Holistic Dentistry for Dentists & Those Desiring Natural Regular Cleanings Verses Going to a Dentist Office

I have developed a non toxic, holistic dental cleaning regimen that save tooth enamel, prevents tooth decay, removes tooth decay and plaque, heals deteriorated gums, removes gingivitis, removes bad breath and whitens teeth in approximately 2 hours for neglected teeth.

Other Published Books

Everything Under Allaah He Rose Above His Throne In A Manner Befitting His Majesty

His saying, "And you should know that Allaah's Messenger ﷺ salla allahu alayhi wa salatul wa salam immeasurable times every nanosecond by the weight of Allah's throne, ink of His words and vast speech for all haneef of all time said, "My nation will divide into 73 sects, all of them in the Fire except one and it is al-Jamaa`ah; the united body upon the truth," Allaah commanded us to unite; to become ijtimaa` upon the truth.

وَاعْتَصِمُوا بِحَبْلِ اللَّهِ جَمِيعًا وَلاَ تَفَرَّقُوا

And cling together to the rope of Allaah and do not separate. Quran (Soorah Aali-Imraan (3), aayah 103)

إِنَّ الَّذِينَ فَرَّقُوا دِينَهُمْ وَكَانُوا شِيَعًا لَسْتَ مِنْهُمْ فِي شَيْءٍ إِنَّمَا أَمْرُهُمْ إِلَى اللَّهِ ثُمَّ يُنَبِّئُهُم بِمَا كَانُوا يَفْعَلُونَ

Those who split up their religion and become sects, you have nothing to do with them. Their affair is just with Allaah. Then He will inform them of what they used to do. Quran (Sooratul An`aam (6), aayah 159)

وَلَا تَكُونُوا كَالَّذِينَ تَفَرَّقُوا وَاخْتَلَفُوا مِن بَعْدِ مَا جَاءَهُمُ الْبَيِّنَاتُ وَأُولَٰئِكَ لَهُمْ عَذَابٌ عَظِيمٌ

And do not be like those who split and differed after the clear signs have come to them. And they are the ones for whom will be a tremendous punishment. Quran (Soorah Aali-Imraan (3), aayah 105) And He, the Most High, said:

وَمَا أَكْثَرُ النَّاسِ وَلَوْ حَرَصْتَ بِمُؤْمِنِينَ

And most of mankind even if you eagerly wish will not be believers. Quran (Soorah Yoosuf (12), aayah 103)

وَمَا وَجَدْنَا لِأَكْثَرِهِم مِّنْ عَهْدٍ وَإِن وَجَدْنَا أَكْثَرَهُمْ لَفَاسِقِينَ

We have not found most of them to be true to their covenant, We have found most of them to be disobedient ones. Quran (Sooratul-A`raaf (7), aayah 102)

So being numerous is not what is counted. What is counted is those who are upon the truth even if they are few in number, even if it is a single person then he will be the Jamaa`ah (the body upon the truth).

His saying, "It was said, "Who are they O Messenger of Allaahﷺ salla allahu alayhi wa salatul wa salam immeasurable times every nanosecond by the weight of Allah's throne, ink of His words and vast speech for all haneef of all time? He ﷺ salla allahu alayhi wa salatul wa salam immeasurable times every nanosecond by the weight of Allah's throne, ink of His words and vast speech for all haneef of all time said, "That which is upon that which I and my companions are upon today."

This is a proper counter terrorism manual compiled from the rulings of the Senior Scholars of Ahlu Sunnah Wal Jummuah hadifullah & global scientists.

This comprehensive outdoor survival manual compiling numerous solutions to many common problems including emergency medicine, weather safe infrastructures, agriculture in polluted areas, good manners and correct belief in Islam.

Sura al Kahf,

The Scholars are The Inheritors of the Prophets ﷺ salla allahu alayhi wa salatul wa salam immeasurable times every nanosecond by the weight of Allah's throne, ink of His words and vast speech for all haneef of all time

Return to the Scholars
Stick with the Main Group of Muslims and Obey The Ruler, Each of you is a Shepherd and he is Responsible for his Flock, The Book of Allaah and the Sunnah of His Messenger ﷺ salla allahu alayhi wa salatul wa salam immeasurable times every nanosecond by the weight of Allah's throne, ink of His words and vast speech for all haneef of all time, Hatred for Terrorism & The Terrorists, All the groups are in the hellfire but one,
Hadeeth on Ad-Dajjal, Final 10 Ayat of Sura Al Kahf, Security & Sustenance, Building Eco Friendly Weather Resistant Homes, How To Make Weather Proof Bricks, How to make Three Different Roof Types, Phytoremediation for air, soil and water, How to remove Lice & parasites, cure ebola and various other diseases.
Information for the public and emergency responders on how to stay safe during public health emergencies. Provided by Centers for Disease Control and Prevention (#CDC).
Get Yours Here may Allah bless you:
https://www.amazon.com/dp/B083F318JM/ref=cm_sw_r_cp_awdb_tl_fGSHEb9DF800H
#CounterTerrorism #EmergencyPreparedness #DisasterRecovery #EmergencyMedicine #WHO #CDC #OutdoorSurvivalGuide #Free #Kindle #KU #Amazon #Holistic Medicine
#Rohinga #Uighur #Kashmiri
AIDS & HIV Cure PSA
{1500 year old ancient cure inside}
The Life and Trials of Imaam Ahmad hadifullah
On the Meaning of Eemaan - Refutation of the Mu'tazilah
Concerning the Falsehood of Ta'weel - Refutation of the Ashariyyah
Concerning the Affirmation of Allaah's Attributes with their Dhaahir and Haqeeqi Meanings
The Consensus of the Companions hadifullah on the Prohibition of Reviling the Rulers and Publicising Their Faults
The Distinguishing Signs of Ahl us-Sunnah
The Distinguishing Signs of Ahl ul-Bidah
The Prohibition of Sitting and Mixing with the Innovators
The Necessity of Accepting the Aahaad Hadeeth - Refutation of the Modernists
Get Yours Here May Allah bless you:
https://www.amazon.com/dp/B0832DHQ2J/ref=cm_sw_r_cp_awdb_tl_zJSHEbVGJT92W

**My Words are Pearls and You Adh Dhaahir al Asma ul Husna,
Al Musawwir, Al Wudud, Al Ghani are the Iridescence of their
Necklace**

*Thareed of Ancient Poetry & Recipes Crunchy, Spicy, Sour, Sweet &
A Little Bit Funky*

Serving Exotic Global Delights in the First Course,

Curried Lotus Root

Spicy, Crunchy Iconic Ambrosia Salad

Blessed, Beautiful Flakiest Pie Crust, Beautiful & Delicious Blood
Orange Salad, Emirati Thareed Laham, Ayran Emirati Drink, Perfect
Pecan Pie, The Pie That'll Make You Cry.

The first course of many pleasurable delicious global cuisine in your
journey while reading the rich history of today and ancient poetry.

Sweet, meltingly-tender recipes with absolute show-stopping poetry
from Ibn Shaddad & fulfilled catering requests for recipes good for
any dinner party fitting anyone's circumstance bringing a fresh take,
a real delight. There are lots of Global offerings.

Tah Dig, Ya'll Dig? Bottom of the Pan Persian Rice, Paratha (Flaky
South Asian Flatbread) Recipe,

Burmese Cinnamon Camel Curry,

Pomegranate Roasted Lamb & Arugula Salad,

Lebanese Baba Ganoush Recipe,

Saucy Saudi Arabian Samboosa with 3 sauces,

Moroccan Beetroot Salad With Yogurt Dressing,

Green Mango Humeidh Salad,

Shingara with 3 sauces,

Emirati Chicken Biryani,

The Hirshon Saudi Arabian Camel Kabsa Pilaf, Kurdi Shifta,
Badischer Zwetschgenkuchen, Kurdish Pilau, Sweet Potato Bua Loy,
Thai Boboa Drink, Turkish Delights, Maleh Salad,

Bright Fresh Tuna & Coriander Salad, Emirati Thareed, Emirati
Chicken Biryani, Dolmas, Middle Eastern Walnut Roasted Red
Pepper Spread, Palestinian Zaatar Mix, Sujuk, Armenian Sweet
Sujuk, Rohingya Curry, Shingara Indian Samosa, Kolija Shingara,
How To Make Chicken Bihari Boti, Burata Mostada, FRIED
CHICKEN SOUP NOODLES,

Persian Lamb in Pomegranate Quince Sauce,

ASH RESHTEH (PERSIAN NOODLE SOUP RECIPE), Kabuli Naan, Persian Pomegranate Soup, SPINACH & YOGURT DIP SABSE BORANI, The Hirshon Emirati Shrimp Fried with Spices, Pakistani Whole Stuffed Camel, Emirati Sulaimani Tea, Doogh, CAMBODIA: NUM KROCH, Persian Lamb and Rhubarb Khoresh, AFGHANI KARAHI RECIPE, Mango Lassi, Fesenjan Persian Chicken Stew with Walnut and Pomegranate Sauce, Crunchy Peanut Butter Spinach, Grilled Xinjiang Lamb Kebabs Recipe with Yogurt, Uyghur Lamb Pilaf (Polo, 羊肉抓饭), LABOO | BEETS IN SYRUP, Red Stew,
CHAI GOL GAVZABAN | BREWED BORAGE TEA,
Red Kidney Beans with Plantains, Fish with Tomatoes & Red Palm oil, Pili- Pili, Uyghur-Style Noodles with Lamb Sauce (Laghman, 新疆拌面), AB DOOGH KHIAR | COLD CUCUMBER AND YOGURT SOUP and so many more offerings.
We end our beautiful & dedicated global journey from seeking out rich exotic ingredients and indigenious tribes' struggles for their safety, security, happiness and very lives to the simplistic delicious staple of my roots recipes.
Serving,
Shepard Pie, Haggis, Afghan Pilau, Halimah's Saffron Honey Lemon Derby Date Night Pie, Creamy American Garlic Cheese Bake and American Derby Pie.
Poetry Community, Poetry Lovers Check me out on Instagram, Food For Foodies dear Poetry Tribe. LA Foodies, Bangkok Foodies, Mumbai Foodies, Food for Foodies, London Foodies, Houston Foodies, all can get a taste.
I hear you Foodies of India forks and knives digging-in.
Best Indian Foodies recipes of all time are found in Where We Go One, We Go All Poetry Community Food for Foodies Series.
#foodies #foodiesofinstagram #foodforfoodies #bandungfoodies #foodiesofindia #mumbaifoodies #londonfoodies #lafoodies #nycfoodies #foodiesunite #barcelonafoodies #houstonfoodies
Matsaman Curry is like a Lover, as Peppery & Fragrant as the Cumin Seed, Its Exciting Allure Will Arouse Your Zawj: Don't Eat the Chicken Bones, Save Them for Your Brothers The Jinn

Serving: Delicious Peanut Salad, Matsaman Curry is like a Lover, as Peppery & Fragrant as the Cumin Seed, Its Exciting Allure Will Arouse Your Zawj, Thai Style Fried Chicken & Malva Pudding. Government, Politics & Diplomacy Grand Old Party: a nickname for the Republican Party GOP or G.O.P
The Republican Party is fighting for a freer and stronger America where everyone has the opportunity to achieve the American Dream, this is the inside scoop on Your Bill of Rights, the script of the US Constitution, Right to Bear Arms, Gun Safety Tips, the history of Persia in Thailand, a few delicious dishes, a study of a few UAE laws and strong evidences from the Quran & Sunnah on obeying

Allaah & His final Messenger ﷺ salla allahu alayhi wa salatul wa salaam ten times immeasurable for all haneef of all time, as well as those placed in authority over you from Muslims & Non Muslim Nations.

Get Yours Here May Allah bless you:
https://www.amazon.com/dp/B085WHV5RC/ref=cm_sw_r_cp_awdb_tl_ZTSHEb6GSZV0Q
#foodies #foodforfoodies #bandungfoodies #foodiesofindia #mumbaifoodies #londonfoodies #lafoodies #nycfoodies #foodiesunite #poetrycommunity #houstonfoodies #bangkokfoodies #Free #KU #Kindle #Amazon

Laa 'ilaaha 'illallaahu wahdahu laa shareeka lahu, lahul-mulku wa lahul-hamdu, wa Huwa 'alaa kulli shay'in Qadeer immeasurable times every nanosecond by the weight of Allah's throne, the ink of His words and vast speech for all haneef of all time: Thriving in America according to the Sunnah Dua, Poetry, Recipes & Politicking

Serving: Lotus, Rose, Cherry & Gooseberry Jam,
Beautiful Pink Blini with Tart Gooseberry-Apple Compote,
Baked Chicken with Sweet & Sour Sauce and lastly
Yummy, Yummy Get In My Tummy My Favorite Go To Comfort Dish, Steamed Chicken.

This exquisite poetry and recipes cook book are the delicious veil you always wanted to peer deeply into, the pages express how to live in the pursuit of happiness for Allaah and Country while feeding you scrumptious meals.

This will shed light on how to start your path to independent financial freedom: purchasing land, building affordable tiny houses and tiny housing complexes, political lobbying and how to lobby congress, how to write a bill and how to ask congress to send your bill into the house.

Get Yours Here May Allah bless you,

#foodies #foodforfoodies #bandungfoodies #foodiesofindia #mumbaifoodies #londonfoodies #lafoodies #nycfoodies #foodiesunite #poetrycommunity #houstonfoodies #FortressoftheMuslim #bangkokfoodies #Free #KU #Kindle #Amazon

"And So, My Fellow Americans Ask Not What Your Country Can Do For You - Ask What You Can Do For God & Your Country."

The New Frontier Rights of Man & God

Serving: Krupenik from Leo Tolstoy's family, Thai Ginger Chicken, Pozharsky Cutlets, Anke pie – Sofya Tolstaya's Sweet Treat, Shirred Eggs – the devilish dish that appears in Mikhail Bulgakov's Master and Margarita, Pasta with Parmesan – Oblomov's favorite dish, How to make goose pate, Goose liver Pate and Roll, Chicken Liver Pate, Cheese Paste, Foie Gras Stuffed Dates, Foie Gras Stuffed Zucchini Flowers and lastly Seared Foie Gras With Mission Fig and Balsamic Reduction.

And so, my fellow Americans: Ask not what your country can do for you - ask what you can do for God & Your country.

Table Of Contents

Discussing

TRANSCRIPT of John F. Kennedy's "New Frontier Speech"

75th anniversary of USS Quincy meeting

The United States and Saudi Arabia: A 75-Year-Long Diplomatic Partnership

OUR PARTNERSHIP ANCHORS PEACE AND STABILITY IN THE MIDDLE EAST

U.S.-SAUDI ECONOMIC TIES ADVANCE PROSPERITY IN BOTH OF OUR NATIONS

History of Max Steineke

Daily Supplications & Dua Fortress of the Muslim

From my heart to yours, get yours here may Allah bless you,

#foodies #foodforfoodies #bandungfoodies #foodiesofindia
#mumbaifoodies #londonfoodies #lafoodies #nycfoodies
#foodiesunite #poetrycommunity #houstonfoodies #bangkokfoodies
#Free #KU #Kindle #Amazon
#FortressoftheMuslim

**I Know Why The Caged Bird Sings: Tea Pot is Whistling
Serving Blue Butterfly Pea Tea with a Dash of Lemon & A
Lavender Sprig**

Serving: Crispy Cajun Shrimp Fettuccine, Hum Bao, Key Lime Pie
& Blue Butterfly pea tea with a dash of lemon and a lavender sprig.
"Meanwhile, let us have a sip of tea. The afternoon glow is
brightening the bamboo, the fountains are bubbling with delight, the
soughing of the pines is heard in our kettle. Let us dream of
evanescence, and linger in the beautiful foolishness of things."
Who would then deny that when I am sipping tea in my tearoom I
am swallowing the whole universe with it and that this very moment
of my lifting the bowl to my lips is eternity itself transcending time
and space?
-D.T. Suzuki
Discussing: Tea Poetry, Wuhan Virus Cover Up,
WHO Sided With China, COVID19, PSA, I Know Why The Caged
Bird Sings by Maya Angelou.
Poetry Community, Poetry Lovers Check me out on Instagram, Food
For Foodies dear Poetry Tribe. LA Foodies, Bangkok Foodies,
Mumbai Foodies, Food for Foodies, London Foodies, Houston
Foodies, all can get a taste.
I hear you Foodies of India forks and knives digging-in.
Best Indian Foodies recipes of all time are found in Where We Go
One, We Go All Poetry Community Food for Foodies Series.
Featuring:
My Words are Pearls and You Adh Dhaahir al Asma ul Husna, Al
Musawwir, Al Wudud, Al Ghani are the Iridescence of their
Necklace: Ancient Poetry & Recipes
Matsaman Curry is like a Lover, as Peppery & Fragrant as the
Cumin Seed, Its Exciting Allure Will Arouse Your Zawj: Don't Eat
the Chicken Bones, Save Them for Your Brothers The Jinn
Laa 'ilaaha 'illallaahu wahdahu laa shareeka lahu, lahul-mulku wa
lahul-hamdu, wa Huwa 'alaa kulli shay'in Qadeer: Thriving in

America according to the Sunnah Dua, Poetry, Recipes &
Politicking
The New Frontier Rights of Man & God
"And So, My Fellow Americans Ask Not What Your Country Can
Do For You - Ask What You Can Do For God & Your Country."
I Know Why The Caged Bird Sings: Tea Pot is Whistling Serving
Blue Butterfly Pea Tea with a Dash of Lemon & A Lavender Sprig
Where We Go One, We Go All Poetry Community Food for Foodies
of Instagram Series. Happy Reading, Cooking, Crying, Eating and
Growing.
Get Yours Today May Allah bless you:

https://www.amazon.com/dp/B08694RTLB/ref=cm_sw_r_cp_awdb_tl_iHIEEbAQFNC8V

#foodies #foodforfoodies #bandungfoodies #foodiesofindia
#mumbaifoodies #londonfoodies #lafoodies #nycfoodies
#foodiesunite #poetrycommunity #houstonfoodies #bangkokfoodies
#Free #KU #Kindle #Amazon

**All Praises are Due to Allah, O Allah as You Have Given Me a
Good Physical Form, so also Favour Me with Good Morals,
Manners and Intelligence immeasurable Times Every
Nanosecond by the weight of His throne, ink of His words and
vast speech for all haneef of all time: Born in the USA Made in
America Food for Foodies of Instagram Series**

The Twilight of Globalization
The Long Hard Road to Decoupling from China
Hanoi-Style Breakfast PHO
New Data Shows U.S. Companies Are Definitely Leaving China
Persian Herb-Stuffed Frittata With Walnuts and Rose Petals (Kuku
Sabzi)
Made in The USA, Born In The USA
Corporate Welfare is Not Free Market Capitalism, We are Against
Cronyism
Pandemic Centers
Dr. Fauci Love Letters to Hillary
Giant Apple and Dulce de Leche Pancake
The Simulation Ran By Bill Gates & 3 Former Harvard University
Teachers Now Arrested For Working Projects for CCP (China)
Population Control
Bill Gates' Father, 'Head' of Planned Parenthood, Inspired His
Abortion, Population Control Views

The newest batch of John Podesta's hacked emails released by Wikileaks shows Obama's transition team kept lists of Muslim and Asian candidates for jobs in the administration
Republican Texas Sen. Ted Cruz Criticized Democrats for Enforcing Stay-at-Home Orders in a way that he Thinks Crosses a Line
Iraqi Eggs with Lamb and Tomatoes (Makhlama Lahm)
Abortion is NOT an Essential During Pandemic
Biscuits with Sawmill Gravy
Scholars have unanimously agreed that it is impermissible and completely prohibited to conduct an abortion if the age of the fetus has reached 120 days
The Difference Between Ittiba (Following) and Al Ibtidah (Innovation) – Imam Ibn Baz
Fatwa Failed Attempt to Abort a Fetus that Died after Delivery
Maldivian Breakfast
Showing Mercy Towards Children is a Means of Achieving the Mercy of Allah: Umm 'Abdillah Al-Waadi'iyyah
Chawanmushi (Japanese Egg Custard)
The Evil Effects of Zinaa' (Fornication) -Transcribed audio
By Shaykh 'Abdullaah 'Ateeq al-Harbee
Turkish Poached Eggs in Yogurt (Cilbir)
The Lawful is clear and the Unlawful is clear, but between them are certain Doubtful things – Sharh as-Sunnah | Dawud Burbank
Kingston Jamaica Curried Chicken
The ill Effects of Sins
Brown Butter Skillet Cake with Berry Compote (Kaiserschmarrn)
Necessity of Approaching Allah with Tawbah and Supplication in Adversity – Imam Ibn Baz
Ful Medames with Hummus
And now for Some Good News,
Low Cost Affordable Housing
EARTHSHIPS
Smorgas
First-Time Handgun Buyers Guide
First-Time Handgun Buyers Guide by NRA Publications Staff
Congee Breakfast of Champions
One Hadeeth
NASI LEMAK WITH BEEF RENDANG

#foodies #foodiesofinstagram #foodforfoodies #bandungfoodies #foodiesofindia #mumbaifoodies #londonfoodies #lafoodies #nycfoodies #foodiesunite #barcelonafoodies #houstonfoodies
The Throne of Allaah Sub Wana ta'ala is A Part of His Majesty,
The Pen Was Made First,
Mankind is Ever Quarrelsome.
Daily Dua & Tawhid The Complete Fortress For The Muslim Hadifullah

Table of Contents:

Ubaadah Ibn Saamit (radiyallaahu `anhu) ascribed to Allaah
Messenger (salla allahu alayhi wa salatul wa salam immeasurable
 times every nanosecond by the weight of Allah's throne, ink of His
words and vast speech for all haneef of all time wherein he said:
'Indeed the first thing that Allaah created was the Pen.' (Reported by
Ahmad 23197. Abu Daawood, 4700. At-Tirmidhee, 2155)
Allaah's Kursi Extends over the Heavens and the Earth
Encompassing Them All – Shaykh Uthaymeen | Dr. Saleh as-Saleh
hadifullah
Speculative Speech (kalaam) about Allaah, the Most High, is an
Innovation and Misguidance
Rhetorical Theology (al-kalaam) & Argumentation, Disputing &
Self-Amazement – Sharh as-Sunnah | Dawud Burbank Hadifullah
The Interesting Dream of the Prophet salla allahu alayhi wa salatul
wa salam immeasurable times every nanosecond by the weight of
Allah's throne, ink of His words and vast speech for all haneef of all
time – Sahih Bukhari hadifullah